Pueblo:
A Pictorial History

Donning Company/Publishers
Norfolk/Virginia Beach

design by Philip Johnson

Enjoy Pursle!
Joanne Dodd

Pueblo
A Pictorial History

by Joanne West Dodds

Contemporary Photographs by Edwin Lloyd Dodds

Edited by Charles S. Pierce, Jr.

*Library of Congress Cataloging-in-
Publication Data*

Dodds, Joanne West, 1944- .
    Pueblo, a pictorial history.
    Bibliography: p.
    Includes index.
    1. Pueblo (Colo.)—Description—Views.
2. Pueblo (Colo.)—History—Pictorial works.
I. Title.
F784.P9D63   1982   978.8'55   82-19775
ISBN 0-89865-281-2 (pbk.)

Printed in the United States of America

Contents

The interior of Charlie Carleton's
store on 3rd Street, currently part of
Rocky Mountain Bank Note Store

Pueblo
A Pictorial History

Foreword

Pueblo, "We Are The Heart"
by Mary Farley

The modern city of Pueblo, Colorado, is the only city in the state of Colorado built on the actual site of a fort. Since the building of the fort the area has been continuously settled. Descendants of the Autobees, Baca, Simpson, and Doyle families still reside in the area. These were the families that formed the early settlements in the county and earned Pueblo the right to call itself Colorado's first breadbasket.

Special people and special events have always been a part of Pueblo. "Uncle" Dick Wooton's buffalo farm represented the first attempt to domesticate the buffalo. Cattle trail pioneer Charles Goodnight housed "Old Blue," who had led the herds from Texas at the Goodnight ranch which was a part of the Mexican Nolan Land Grant. The first Fourth of July celebration in the state was in Pueblo, according to O. J. Goldrick. And, the Mormon Battalion, part of the United States Army participating in the Mexican War was wintered here in Pueblo.

These are just a few of the memorable events that set Pueblo apart from other communities. I urge every Puebloan to be proud of their town and to actively support the preservation of its heritage.

Acknowledgments

Pueblo is not my home by birth. I come from a lovely community but one where you remain a stranger to those you meet. Pueblo has become my home among friends. As the local history librarian for the Pueblo Library District, I asked Puebloans for help in preserving the community's history. Not once did a Puebloan tell me no. At this time I wish to thank each of you publicly. Your contributions to Pueblo's heritage will help others as they have helped me.

A few individuals should be mentioned by name. First, always, is my husband Edwin Lloyd Dodds, a patient man, who in addition to doing much of the copy work for the book carried a 4 x 5 camera around Pueblo for months taking photographs. Next come my friends, in alphabetical order so that they will remain my friends; Steve Eller (copy work), Marilyn McLaughlin (layout), Jim Munch (architectural survey), Ed Simonich (oral histories), John Smith (photograph identification), and Noreen Stringfellow (typing and church research). John Suhay and Gladys Hassey must be acknowledged for allowing me to use some of the historic photographs they have preserved. Both have contributed significantly to Pueblo's heritage by their efforts.

Mrs. John B. (Mary) Farley has done more to preserve Pueblo's history than any other individual I know. She has always been willing to share her knowledge with me. Her advice and counsel on the early years of Pueblo are a part of this book. Ralph Taylor has given Pueblo's history his loving attention for many years. Known by many as Mr. Pueblo History, Mr. Taylor has been generous to the library and to me. Lastly, I wish to acknowledge the entire Pueblo Library District staff. Every member of the staff has contributed to the book in some way. Charles E. Bates, the director, deserves special thanks.

The photographs in this pictorial history of Pueblo are based on the collection of the Western Research Room of the Pueblo Library District.

Chapter One
Beginnings

Plains Indians Camp

The Fountain and Arkansas rivers created natural trails. Native Americans camped along their banks for generations. Some of the tribes known to have lived in the Pueblo area were the Arapahoe, Ute, Pawnee, Comanche, Apache, and Kiowa. This undated photograph is identified only as a Plains Indian scene. Photograph courtesy of the Library of Congress

**San Carlos de los Jupes
Historical Marker**

*T*ales told of Spanish explorers criss-crossing the southern plains of Colorado, once considered to be fables, are now being proven true. The Comanche settlement known as San Carlos de los Jupes is Pueblo County's testimony to her early Hispanic heritage. Founded in 1787 under the direction of Juan Bautista de Anza, governor of New Mexico, this Comanche settlement was a part of Spanish colonial policy to civilize the native population. Comanche religious beliefs caused abandonment of the village because a member of the tribe died there. The village of San Carlos de los Jupes should also be remembered for the two leaders associated with its creation: Juan Bautista de Anza, the founder of San Francisco, California, and Cuerno Verde, the Comanche leader who fought to preserve the ways of his people. *Photograph courtesy of the Pueblo Library District*

Fort Pueblo

*T*his 1959 painting of Fort Pueblo by Jolan B. Truan was based on descriptions of the fort by early travelers. Fort Pueblo was a civilian fort established by independent traders. Built in 1842 by adobe masons from, we believe, Taos, Fort Pueblo was a trading center along the boundary between Mexico and the United States. A list of the early residents includes George Simpson, Robert Fisher, Alexander Barclay, Mathew Kinkead, Francisco Conn, Joseph Mantz, "Uncle" Dick Wootton, Teresita Suaso, and James P. Beckwourth. In his journal, Beckwourth records the naming of the fort. He says "we gave it the name of Pueblo."

Other Colorado forts of the era were named for individuals, such as Fort Bent, Fort Vasquez, or later Fort Lyon and Fort Garland. It seems that the men who founded Fort Pueblo recognized it as a collective project. The selection of the Spanish word pueblo, which means "village," reinforces the concept of community.

On Christmas Day 1854, a band of Utes led by Blanco massacred the occupants of the fort. Jose Ignacio Valencia, Juan Rafael Medina, Guadalupe Vigil, Francisco Mestas, Juan Blas Martin, Benito Sandoval, Juan Aragon, Tanislado de Luna, and Manuel Lucero were killed. Chepita Miera, Felix and Juan Isidro Sandoval were taken captives. Felix and Juan were later returned to their families, but Chepita was killed. *Photograph courtesy of the Pueblo Library District*

16

Charles Autobees, 1864

Colorado's earliest settlements endured an unsettled political and stubborn natural environment. Here where the United States and Mexico sought control of their border fringes, large Mexican land grants were bestowed upon those pledging to colonize and secure the untenanted land. Among the earliest settlers was Charles Autobees, who in 1846 secured part of the Nolan Grant at the site of the Taos Trail crossing at the San Carlos River seven miles south of Pueblo. Moving on February 20, 1853, to the confluence of the Huerfano and Arkansas rivers, he was joined by Richard Wootton and Joseph B. Doyle in building their placitas composed of adobe living quarters, blacksmith shops, and storage rooms, outside of which stood the ovens and corrals. Sixteen miles south of this point, Doyle established his Casa Blanca in 1859. Photograph courtesy of the Cragin Collection, Pioneers' Museum, Colorado Springs

The beginnings of Pueblo County are linked to the evolving territorial rights of several groups. First were the nomadic Native American tribes. Conquistadors from Spain then claimed the land in the European tradition. In the seventeenth and eighteenth centuries Spain drew no nothern boundary. The province stretched as far to the north as periodic military expeditions could enforce. The Mexican government assumed possession of the territory following the war of independence from Spain, 1810 to 1821. Colonists from northern New Mexico were the first permanent residents under the land grant system. Citizens of the United States, first as fur trappers and later as traders, were the next group to establish settlements. The legal transfer of the land to the United States occurred in two parts. The 1803 Louisiana Purchase transferred the area north and east of the Arkansas River to the United States. The remaining portion was annexed following the Mexican War, 1846 to 1848.

Mariano Autobees and Elena Baca

The continued occupation of the Pueblo area by the Baca and Autobees families indicates that Pueblo was not abandoned after the massacre.

Mariano, shown here with his wife, Elena Baca, was born October 15, 1837, in Taos to Charles Autobees and Serafina Avila. Elena was the daughter of Marcelino Baca and Tomasa, a Pawnee. Photograph courtesy of Richad Luna

HERE THE HISTORIC ARKANSAS RIVER WAS THE INTERNATIONAL BOUNDARY BETWEEN THE UNITED STATES AND SPAIN, LATER BETWEEN THE U.S. AND THE REPUBLIC OF MEXICO UNTILL 1848. MEXICO BESTOWED LARGE LAND GRANTS TO THOSE WHO PROMISED TO COLONIZE ITS NORTHERN BORDERLANDS AND PROMOTE AGRICULTURE AND THE ARTS. AMONG THE GRANTS WAS THE VIGIL AND SAINT VRAIN THAT ONCE ENCOMPASSED ALL OF WHAT THE EYE CAN SEE TO THE SOUTH. HERE IT WAS THAT ST. LOUIS BORN FRENCH TRAPPER, TRADER, AND FARMER CHARLES AUTOBEES CAME ON FEBRUARY 20, 1853 TO FOUND HIS SETTLEMENT ON THE WEST BANK OF THE HUERFANO RIVER TWO MILES SOUTH OF ITS JUNCTION WITH THE ARKANSAS. QUICKLY CHANNELING IRRIGATION DITCHES, HE AND HIS COMPANIONS SOON HAD THE BOTTOM LAND PRODUCING GARDEN VEGETABLES. SOON AFTER, HE WAS JOINED DOWNSTREAM BY OTHERS WHO TOOK AN EARLY LIKING TO THIS UPPER ARKANSAS VALLEY, INCLUDING JOSEPH B. DOYLE, WILLIAM KROENIG, AND ALSO BY UNCLE DICK WOOTTON WHOSE LOG ENCLOSED PLACITA WAS A BASTION AGAINST UTE INDIANS RAIDS. SAFELY WITHIN THE PICKET WALL WERE THE LIVING QUARTERS, BLACKSMITH SHOP, WAGON SHOP, AND STORAGE ROOMS. DURING THE FIRST FIVE YEARS, AUTOBEES WATCHED COLONISTS COME AND GO FROM THESE SURROUNDINGS UNTIL THE PIKES PEAK GOLD RUSH ESTABLISHED THE AREA AS AN IMPORTANT PROVISIONER OF FOOD TO KEEP THE RUSH ALIVE. IN 1861, HIS SETTLEMENT BECAME THE COUNTY SEAT WITH AUTOBEES, HIMSELF, A COMMISSIONER. THE TOWN SERVED UNTIL HIS DEATH IN 1882 AND THE BUILDINGS DISAPPEARED IN A FLOOD SOME YEARS LATER. TODAY, MANY OF THE AUTOBEES, ORTIVIS, TOBIN, JAQUES, SIERRA, FINN, OLGUIN, AND BACA FAMILY MEMBERS ARE DECENDENTS OF THOSE EARLY ARRIVALS INCLUDING CHARLES AUTOBEES.

ERECTED BY THE STATE HISTORICAL SOCIETY OF COLORADO AND THE ARKANSAS VALLEY CHAPTER OF THE DAUGHTERS OF THE AMERICAN REVOLUTION THROUGH THE ROBERT S. ELLISON MEMORIAL FUND, 1976.

Autobees' Settlement Historical Marker

During the transition period from Mexican rule to American rule many northern New Mexico families settled along the rich river lands. By the 1870 United States Census, one-fourth of the residents of Pueblo County were Hispanic. Autobees' settlement was the center of the Hispanic agricultural community. Photograph courtesy of the Pueblo Library District

Reconstruction of Pike's Stockade

Legal transfer of the region to the government of the United States began with the Louisiana Purchase in 1803. Following the acquisition of the area from France, two exploration teams were sent west. The Lewis and Clark Expedition, 1804-06, explored the northern portion, and the Zebulon Pike Expedition explored the southern portion.

It was from Pueblo on November 24, 1806, that Zebulon Pike began his famous attempt to climb Pike's Peak. The main portion of his party was left at the fork of the Arkansas and Fountain rivers. To protect his men, fourteen trees were cut down and a stockade was built. Pike's Pueblo stockade is believed to be the first structure built by citizens of the United States in Colorado. Today, this reconstruction of the stockade reminds those in the city hall area of Pueblo's heritage. Photograph courtesy of the Pueblo Library District

Mormon Battalion Camp at Pueblo, 1847

From August 7, 1846, to May 1847 a community of Mormons wintered east of Pueblo in the river bottom of the Arkansas River. At one point the population reached 275. According to diary records, a meeting hall was built and regular church services were held. During May 1847 all but two of the Mormon families traveled on to Utah. Drawing from the diary of John Brown; photograph courtesy of the Pueblo Library District

Spanish Peaks, 1853

The war with Mexico, 1846-48, concluded the legal transfer of the area to the United States. Beginning in 1806, a series of exploration parties passed through Pueblo County. They included the Stephen H. Long Expedition in 1820, Lieutenant John C. Fremont's expeditions in 1843-44, 1845, and 1848, and Captain John W. Gunnison's Expedition in 1853. This illustration by J. M. Stanley of the Wah-ha-ta-gas or Spanish Peaks is from Gunnison's Expedition. The main purpose of this expedition was to ascertain the most practical and economical route for a railroad from the Mississippi River to the Pacific Ocean. Illustration courtesy of the Pueblo Library District

300 Block of Santa Fe Avenue, 1880

An article from the Pueblo Chieftain *in 1878 stated:*

"The cowboy is apt to spend his money liberally when he gets paid off after his long drive from Texas, and the pimps, gamblers and prostitutes generally manage to get to the point where the boys are paid off so as to give them a good chance to invest their money in fun.

The people do not look with favor on the advent of these classes, and only tolerate them because they cannot well help themselves. They follow the annual cattle drive like vultures follow an army, and disappear at the end of the cattle driving and shipping season. It is this

Chapter Two
Agriculture and Cowboys: the First Trade Era

feature of the business that makes people
averse to the Texas business coming to
their towns.''
    The Arkansas Hall on Santa Fe Avenue
behind the cowboys was Alfred L. Run-
yan's favorite bar. Photograph courtesy
of the Pueblo Library District

Wagon Train Fording the Arkansas River, 1860s

In the period from 1858 to 1860 gold was discovered in quantity in Colorado. Thousands of miners lined the trails to Colorado. Businessmen were quick to recognize the need for supplies, and towns were built. Fountain City, northeast of the confluence of the Fountain Creek and the Arkansas River, was founded in 1858. Photograph courtesy of the Pueblo Library District

Colonel A. G. Boone

Colonel Albert Gallatin Boone, a grandson of Daniel Boone, founded the town of Boone in 1860 or 1861. In 1861 he was appointed special commissioner by the United States government to negotiate a treaty with the Cheyenne and Arapahoe. It was concluded at Bent's Fort and was known as the Boone Treaty. The reservation existed until the treaty of Little Arkansas in 1865. Photograph courtesy of the Pueblo Library District

In the period from 1858 to 1860 gold was discovered in quantity in Colorado. As a result, thousands of miners followed the trails to Colorado. Businessmen were quick to recognize the need for supplies and towns began. Fountain City, northeast of the confluence of Fountain Creek and the Arkansas River, was founded in 1858 and platted the following spring by two engineers named Shaffer and Brown. Pueblo, located west of Fountain Creek and north of the Arkansas River, began in the winter of 1859 and the early spring of 1860. Agricultural products and cattle furnished food for the mining settlements and thus provided the first economic foundations for the community.

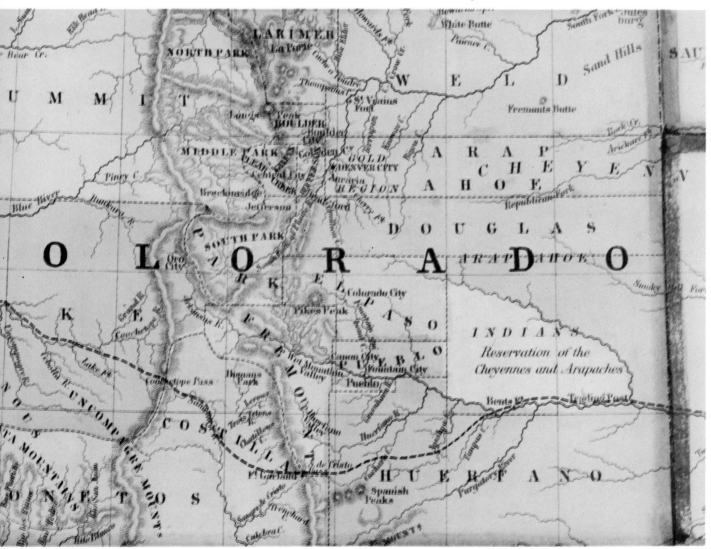

Map of Pueblo County Identifying the Site of the Cheyenne and Arapahoe Reservation, circa 1870

From the 1846 appointment of Thomas Fitzpatrick as Indian agent, to the November 1864 Sand Creek Massacre of the Cheyenne Indians, the native American population steadily decreased in Pueblo County. (Company G from Pueblo was a part of John M. Chivington's regiment.) The 1870 United States Census records no native Americans in Pueblo County. This 1861 map locates the Cheyenne and Arapahoe Indian reservation which was a part of the Boone Treaty. Photograph courtesy of the Pueblo Library District

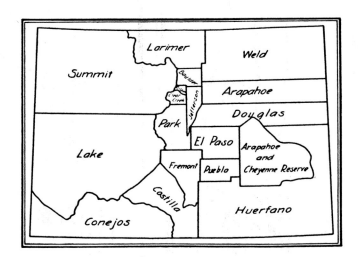

Colorado's Original Seventeen Counties

*T*he territory of Colorado was created by act of Congress February 28, 1861. Pueblo County was one of the original seventeen counties. From 1861 to 1865 Pueblo County's eastern boundary was the Arapahoe and Cheyenne reservation. Map courtesy of the University of Colorado Studies, *volume 3, number 4, August, 1906*

Fort Reynolds Historical Marker

*P*art of the fear of living on the frontier was the lack of protection. Fort Reynolds was an attempt on the part of the United States military to address that danger. The fort, built of adobe, was located on the south side of the Arkansas River along present U.S. Highway 50. In use from 1867 to 1872, the fort protected the area between Fort Lyon and Fort Garland. In 1870 the total population of Fort Reynolds was fifty-four. There were four officers and nine women and children, leaving forty-one soldiers. Fifty percent of the soldiers were foreign born. Photograph courtesy of the Pueblo Library District

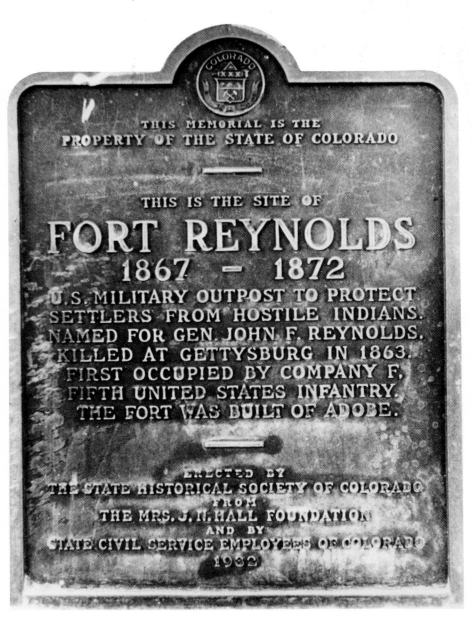

THIS MEMORIAL IS THE
PROPERTY OF THE STATE OF COLORADO

THIS IS THE SITE OF

FORT REYNOLDS
1867 – 1872
U.S. MILITARY OUTPOST TO PROTECT
SETTLERS FROM HOSTILE INDIANS.
NAMED FOR GEN. JOHN F. REYNOLDS,
KILLED AT GETTYSBURG IN 1863.
FIRST OCCUPIED BY COMPANY F,
FIFTH UNITED STATES INFANTRY.
THE FORT WAS BUILT OF ADOBE.

ERECTED BY
THE STATE HISTORICAL SOCIETY OF COLORADO
FROM
THE MRS. J. N. HALL FOUNDATION
AND BY
STATE CIVIL SERVICE EMPLOYEES OF COLORADO
1932

Kit Carson, 1867

This photograph of Kit Carson (seated, left), taken by Civil War photographer Mathew Brady, was probably the last photograph taken of him. Ute relocation problems had sent him to Washington for meetings with D.C. Oaks (standing left); Lafayette Head, superintendent of Indian Affairs (standing right); and Hiram P. Bennett, Colorado Territorial Representative (seated right). Photograph courtesy of the Public Library District

The Will of Christopher "Kit" Carson, 1868

The first edition of the Colorado Chieftain *contained a notice of Kit Carson's death (May 23, 1868) in Pueblo County at Fort Lyon. This is a facsimile of the first page of his will. The only portion of the will in Carson's handwriting is his signature. Facsimile of the will courtesy of the Pueblo Library District*

Filed in Probate Court, June 1, 1868
M.S. Bradford, Judge

Fort Lyon
Pueblo County.
Colorado Territory.
May 15th 1868.

I, Christopher Carson, a resident of Pueblo County, Colorado Territory, knowing the uncertainty of life, and being now of sound mind, do make this, my last will and Testament.

To wit

<u>First.</u> It is my will, that of my cattle, numbering from one hundred to two hundred head, such only, shall be sold, from time to time, as may be necessary for the support of my children; The balance to be retained, with the increase, for the benefit of my children.

<u>Secondly.</u> It is my will, that my seven yoke of steers and two ox wagons, shall be kept by my Administrator, for the use and support of my children.

<u>Thirdly.</u> It is my will, that my four horses and one carriage, shall be kept by my Administrator for the use and support of my children.

Joseph Bainbridge Doyle

Joseph Bainbridge Doyle, one of the founders of Fort Pueblo, founded the community of Doyle. He purchased two square miles of the Huerfano Valley in 1859 from Cornelio Vigil and Ceran St. Vrain and established his family in the large ranch house known as Casa Blanca. Doyle brought 600 acres under cultivation, built irrigation ditches, established one of the first flour mills in Colorado, and established Pueblo County as Colorado's first agricultural community. Photograph courtesy of the Pueblo Library District

Oscar J. Goldrick

Honored as the first teacher in Colorado, Goldrick was brought to Doyle, Colorado, to tutor Doyle's children. During the gold rush he moved to Denver. Photograph courtesy of the Colorado Historical Society

Pueblo County's Borders in 1868

In 1868 the legislature reduced Huerfano County to its modern irregular bounds and increased Pueblo County's eastern boundary to the Kansas border. Map courtesy of the University of Colorado Studies, *vol. 3, number 4, August, 1906*

In the winter of 1859-60 cabins were constructed in what was to become Pueblo. One account locates the cabins in the vicinity of First Street and Santa Fe Avenue, and another account states that the first cabin was built by A. W. "Jack" Wright at the rear of the northeast corner of what is now Fourth Street and Santa Fe Avenue. There is also a discrepancy about who was present at the founding of Pueblo.

The records of the Southern Colorado Pioneers Association identify the following persons as being present at the meeting to organize a town on May 22, 1860: Jack Allen, John Kearns, Albert Bercaw, W. H. Ricker, Dr. Catterson, Wesley Catterson, Ed Cozzens, A. C. Wright, Mrs. A. C. Wright, and Mrs. Mary Simms. Other records add the names of Dr. Belt, Cy Warren, and W. H. Green. On July 1, 1860, the town was formally laid out and named in honor of the old fort. (Adobe bricks from the fort had been used by some of the new residents for their dwellings.)

The town was surveyed by Beul and Boyd of Denver. Green and Bercaw built the first bridge over the Arkansas River. The first store was established in 1859 at the mouth of the Fountain River by Cooper and Wing. Aaron Sims kept the first hotel. Mail service, weekly from Denver, began in 1862, the same year that John A. Thatcher came to town.

St. Peter's Episcopal Church was the first church erected in Pueblo. Built on the corner of Seventh Street and Santa Fe Avenue, it was constructed in 1868 of adobe brick. Used not only by Episcopalians, St. Peter's was a church for the whole community. Illustration courtesy of the Pueblo Library District

Santa Fe Avenue, Circa 1868

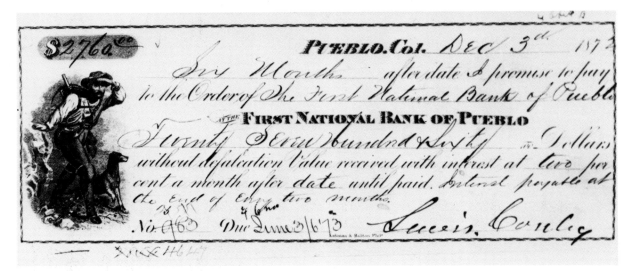

First National Bank of Pueblo Check, 1872

In the Colorado Territory poll book for the August 1861 election, the community was identified as "Pueblo of the Arkansas River." The election district consisted of "that area drained by the Arkansas, Del Norte, and San Juan Rivers." All votes were given by the voters in person, viva voce *or handed in writing to the judges and recorded by the clerk. The Hispanic vote was difficult to identify because of the English spelling of names, but over 28 percent could be identified as Hispanic. Some of the English names were also misspelled, such as Van Daniel Boone listed as V. D. Boon. This 1872 First National Bank of Pueblo check honors the role of the gold rush in Pueblo's history. Illustration courtesy of First National Bank*

Those seeking office:
Hiran P. Bennet vs. B. D. Williams
R. B. Willis vs. I. Francisco
Mat Riddleberger vs. G. M. Chilcott

The Pueblo of the Arkansas River male residents who voted in the 1861 election. (The names are listed as they appeared.)

W. H. Chapman	G. M. Chilcott	Antonio Sandival	Francisco Fredrico
William Ricker	William Williams	V. D. Boon	Joquin Checon
G. H. Chapman	Roca Mayah	Wm. S. Catterson	Augustine Fernandes
Abram Mayhood	Pedro Martin	Jose Barrados	Savereno Rodecins
W. R. Fowler	Antonio Gabadoon	C. W. Warren	Ciatan Lava
W. Cummens	L. B. Lockhart	Nicholas George	Carmicean Traval
Aaron Sims	J. F. Smith	Serapheme Cassera	Marian Barnard
P. L. Moro	Rufus Paine	Cariphence Malaskas	Juan De La Cruz
J. R. Lampkin	I. W. Roggers	O. G. Darwub	John Allen
G. Morris	R. G. Williams	I. W. Martine	Ernest Chadet
S. S. Smith	Juan Cantana	H. W. Crefswell	Lorenzo Ramero
J. W. Catterson	Lenard Johnston	John Cassady	Husto Gangallas
J. F. Cooper	Decidero Drego	D. McIntire	Carmel Morino
D. P. Wright	Decidero Schwartzo	James Brumfield	Juan Jesus Lava
A. C. Wright	Pero Ramero	Hickory Roggers	Robert Douglas
		F. A. White	Juan Trujillo
		C. H. Randal	Mariano Gomas
		C. W. Sepians	Jesus Romaro
		C. H. Hall	Juan Vahill
		J. B. Andrews	
		C. C. Peck	
		C. M. Hannam	
		C. S. Cornforth	
		H. S. Carnes	

Two Views of Santa Fe Avenue

Pueblo County was organized in 1862. The first board of county commissioners included Richard L. Wootton, W. H. Chapman, and O. H. P. Baxter, chairman. The first appointed sheriff was Henry Way, the first elected sheriff, John B. Rice. The first appointed and elected county clerk was Stephen Smith. William Chapman was the first elected probate judge.

The first district judge, Allen A. Bradford, was appointed at a time of unrest due to the slavery question. Bradford was given a military escort to Pueblo, which was reputed to be a Southern stronghold. Bradford accepted the escort, although "he was only a little afraid" (from the H. H. Bancroft interviews).

Pueblo was organized as a town under the laws of the Colorado Territory by the board of county commissioners on March 22, 1870. George A. Hinsdale, Mark G. Bradford, James Rice, Henry C. Thatcher, and Henry R. Cooper were appointed trustees by the county commissioners.

The first town election was held on Monday, April 4, 1870. The first elected trustees were George A. Hinsdale, Lewis Conley, Sam McBride, C. P. Peabody, and O. H. P. Baxter.

Two early views of Santa Fe Avenue circa 1867 represent the rapid growth along Pueblo's first business district. Photograph courtesy of the Pueblo Library District

Michael Beshoar

Dr. Michael Beshoar published the first issue of the Colorado Chieftain *on June 1, 1868. On March 10, 1869, he sold the newspaper to Sam McBride, who had been the typesetter. John J. Lambert became the third owner in June 1870 while he was still quartermaster at Fort Reynolds. Under Lambert's direction in 1872 a daily titled the* Pueblo Chieftain *was begun. Today the* Pueblo Chieftain *is one of the oldest newspapers in Colorado still being published. Photograph courtesy of the Pueblo Library District*

Pueblo's First Jail

In 1869 Morgan, Barndollar, Mullaly, and Moses Anker established the brickyards.

The county jail was the first orthodox burned-brick structure in Pueblo, and lacked windows. Photograph courtesy of the Pueblo Library District

The Adobe Centennial School After It Had Been Abandoned

The first school in Pueblo was located at 421 North Santa Fe Avenue. George Bilby is traditionally believed to have been the first teacher in town. Miss Clara Weston was another early teacher. During the summer of 1864 she taught a summer school in the new frame building. As there were no bridges across the Fountain River at that time, she took off her shoes and waded the stream twice a day for four months.

School District No. 1 was formally organized in 1866, with L. R. Graves, president; H. C. Thatcher, secretary; and D. Sheets, treasurer.

In 1870 the Adobe Centennial School was opened. Photograph courtesy of the Pueblo Library District

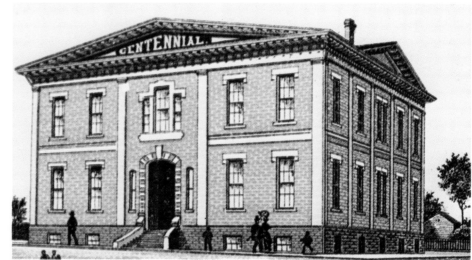

The Second Centennial School, circa 1880

"Have you seen Sam?" was the August 17, 1876, headline of the Chieftain. *It continued with the news that Sam McBride, treasurer of the school board and former owner of the* Chieftain, *had left for the national Democratic convention in St. Louis in June 1876 with $14,000 of school funds and had not returned. Sam had been well liked, and reporters had been reluctant to announce the news of*

Sam's action. Money was borrowed at 10 percent to complete the building.

The bondsmen were freed from replacing the lost funds due to a technicality. This second Centennial School was opened January 9, 1878. Centennial School was named in honor of Colorado gaining statehood during the centennial of the United States. Photograph courtesy of the Pueblo Library District

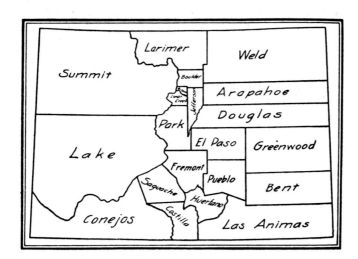

Pueblo County's Borders in 1870

In 1870 the Eighth Assembly created Greenwood and Bent counties from portions of El Paso and Pueblo counties, and Pueblo County's existing boundaries were established. Map courtesy of the University of Colorado Studies, vol. 3, no. 4, August, 1906

Annie Blake

All of Pueblo south of the Arkansas River, as well as the land between the St. Charles River and the Greenhorn Mountains was owned at one time by Mrs. Annie Blake. The entire Gervacio Nolan Mexican Land Grant was purchased by Mrs. Blake for $10,000 in 1869. She sold one-third interest to Charles Goodnight for $5,000 and one-third to Peter Dotson for $5,000. Dotson settled along the St. Charles River southeast of Beulah, and Goodnight headquartered five miles west of South Pueblo on the Arkansas River.

Annie Blake was an exceptional woman. In 1870 only eight Pueblo County women were employed in positions outside their homes. Three were housekeepers and five were domestic servants. Photograph courtesy of the Colorado Historical Society

Charles Goodnight

Charles Goodnight and Oliver Loving established the Goodnight-Loving cattle trail from the Pecos River through Trinidad, Pueblo, Colorado Springs, and Denver to Cheyenne, Wyoming, in 1866. Goodnight acquired a portion of the Nolan Mexican Land Grant in 1869 for his Rock Canon Ranch. Located west of South Pueblo in a sheltered valley, where the Arkansas River cuts through a narrow rock canyon, this was to be the home of his bride-to-be.

On July 26, 1870, Charles Goodnight married Mary Ann Dyer in Hickman, Kentucky. After the ceremony they took the boat to St. Louis, and from there they journeyed to Abilene, Kansas, by rail. After a night at the Drover's Hotel they left by stage for Pueblo. Mrs. Goodnight's first night in Pueblo was spent at the Drover's Hotel run by Mr. and Mrs. Harry Pickard. The next morning two men were found swinging from a telegraph pole. Mr. Goodnight tried to hide the event from his bride but Mrs. Pickard told Mary. When confronted with the truth, Mr. Goodnight, not being accustomed to making excuses, replied, "Well, I don't think it hurt the telegraph pole." Photograph courtesy of the Pueblo Library District

Goodnight Barn

The Goodnight Barn, constructed of limestone blocks, was placed on the National Register of Historic Places in 1974. Photograph courtesy of Edwin L. Dodds

Santa Fe Avenue, Spring 1870

Stockgrowers National Bank, 1888

In September 1873 Charles Goodnight and others organized the Stockgrowers National Bank. The building still stands and is located on the corner of Third Street and Santa Fe Avenue. A financial panic wiped Goodnight out and he left the area. Photograph courtesy of the Pueblo Library District

This is what the west side of Santa Fe Avenue between Fourth and Fifth streets looked like in the spring of 1870. The building on the left was the X-10-U-8 Saloon, and the building in the center was the book and shoe store of Dr. J. W. O. Snyder. Dr. Snyder was the postmaster in 1870 and had the post office in his store. The one-story building on the right was the office of A. A. Bradford and Henry C. Thatcher, prominent lawyers, and in it court was held.

It was along Santa Fe Avenue in 1870 that the colony of German settlers led by Carl Wulstein stopped so that their caravan of some seventy wagons might be viewed by the populace. They traveled on to the Wet Mountain Valley, where the community of Colfax was laid out.

The original post office was kept by Aaron Sims, and next by D. J. Hayden in his store, opened in 1863. Wilbur F. Stone gives the following description of the mail service: "The mail bag, when it arrived, was unceremoniously emptied in the middle of the floor and the crowd invited to pitch in, such as could read, and pick out what belonged to them. What was left after this promiscuous sorting, was put in an empty candle box, and when the people came to the post office, they were directed to 'go and look for themselves and not bother the postmaster.'" Photograph courtesy of the Pueblo Library District

Mexican Settlement, 1888

The story of Juan "Chiquito" Trujillo, who lived in an adobe house on the Fountain City side of the Arkansas River, is a romantic tale. Juan had fallen in love with a young women living at the Mexican settlement at Doyle's ranch. Not being kindly received by her family, he met her in a clandestine manner. One day the lovers decided that Juan should meet her at a certain time and place and whisk her off to his home on the Fountain Creek.

Their plans were followed according to schedule, but the eloping lovers were no sooner on their way than their purpose was discovered by her father. Soon he and his friends were in hot pursuit. Juan and companion arrived at his home shortly before their pursuers did. The surrender of the stolen daughter was demanded, and Juan refused. Barricading his door, Juan prepared to give battle. The attacking group fired round after round to no avail into the adobe while Juan, using one small window as a loophole, struck terror in the ranks. All day the battle raged. Finally wearied with the uselessness of continuing to try to shoot through the thick adobe walls, the pursuers withdrew and returned home. This 1888 drawing of the adobe dwellings on the Fountain City side of the river may well have included Juan Trujillo's home. By the 1870 United States Census, one-fourth of the residents of Pueblo County were Hispanic. Photograph courtesy of the Pueblo Library District

Henry C. Thatcher

Henry C. Thatcher, brother of John and Mahlon Thatcher, at the age of thirty-four became the first chief justice of the state of Colorado. He retired from the Colorado Supreme Court to join the firm of Adams and Gast. He died in 1884 at the age of forty-two. Photograph courtesy of the Pueblo Library District

Tom Watson, Pioneer Cowboy

Santa Fe Avenue was Pueblo's main business district in the 1870s. Old-timers remember the afternoon when a group of cowboys, while cantering down the avenue, came to a sign proclaiming "Painless Dentistry." For entertainment they emptied their guns into it. Then one of the company dismounted and went in to get a sore tooth treated. The dentist was a quiet-looking young man. "See here," shouted the cowboy as he advanced toward the chair," I want a tooth fixed, and I don't want any hightoned prices charged either." He threw himself into the chair, laid his gun across his lap, and told the dentist that if he hurt him he would shoot the top of his head off.

"Very well," replied the dentist. "However you must take gas for this is a bad tooth and will give trouble." The cowboy swore, but finally yielded. Presently he was insensible. The dentist pulled the tooth and then before his patient regained consciousness, he securely tied him hand and foot to the chair. Then taking the cowboy's gun, the dentist took up his position where the patient could see him when he came to. As the cowboy struggled back to consciousness, the first thing he saw was the dentist pointing the revolver at him, and saying, "Now, don't move. Just open your mouth as wide as possible and I will shoot the bad tooth off." The cowboy yelled for mercy. On the condition that the cowboy would restore the sign outside the office, the dentist cut his bonds. After paying the five dollars for the tooth, the cowboy departed with a new opinion of dentists. This story was published in Field and Farm, *February 9, 1895. Tom Watson, pictured here on his horse may have been one of the cowboys who told this story. Photograph courtesy of the Pueblo Library District*

36

First Pueblo County Courthouse, 1866-1872

The first Pueblo County Courthouse, from 1866 to 1872, was located at Third Street and Santa Fe Avenue or 228 North Santa Fe Avenue. The building had been purchased from Stephen Smith, who had erected it in the middle of Third Street because his claim to a lot as one of the first residents of the town had been overlooked due to his absence from town at that time. Finding, upon his return, that the desirable lots had all been assigned and that nothing remained for him, he erected his building in the middle of Third Street. The first lawful court was held about 1862, by Judge Bradford. Si Smith was the United States marshal. Photograph courtesy of the Pueblo Library District

Second County Courthouse, 1872-1912

The second county courthouse was completed in 1872 at Tenth and Main streets. It was built without cost to the taxpayers, as it was financed from the sale of lots in a quarter section of land which had been preempted by the county and filed as a city addition.

The court was constituted by an act which went into effect March 5, 1881, for the district consisting of Pueblo, Bent, Las Animas, and Huerfano counties, and was known as the third district. The Eighth General Assembly in redistricting the state formed the tenth district, consisting of Pueblo and Otero counties. The county court was established by act in March 1877, and went into force June 20, 1877. M. J. Galligan was the presiding judge. The criminal court was established in 1883, with Judge Thomas T. Player presiding. Photograph courtesy of the Pueblo Library District

J. N. Carlile Hose Company, No. 2, Circa 1880

Pueblo's fire protection began with bucket brigades. At the sound of the fire alarm every able-bodied citizen grabbed a bucket and proceeded with haste to the scene of the action. The James Rice Hose Company was Pueblo's first formally organized fire company. In February 1873 the company purchased a used fire truck from Denver for $600. By April uniforms ordered from New York had arrived. The J. A. Richardson Hose Company was organized the next year, and the newly

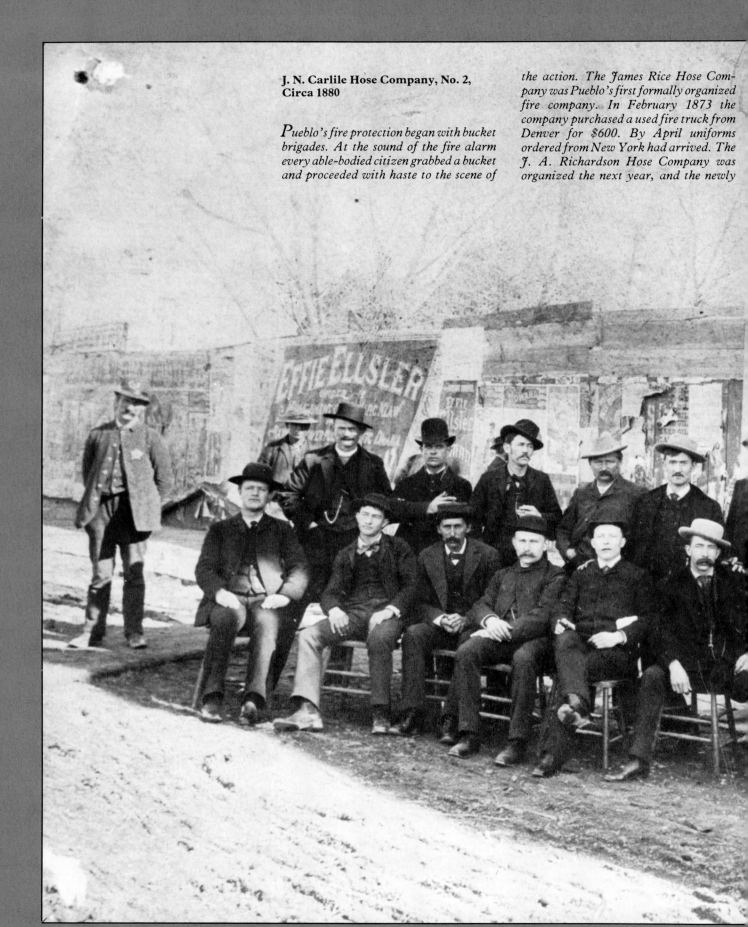

purchased Silsby hose carts were being used.

Numerous volunteers were needed to pull and operate the hand pumps and hose wagons. Leading citizens who never ran for public office, such as Samual Gallup, participated in the companies. Competitions between towns were popular. It was not until the mid 1880s that steam pumps pulled by horses began to replace hand pumps. The steam pumps required fewer people to operate them. *Photograph courtesy of the Pueblo Library District*

View of Pueblo Which Appeared in a December 1880 Issue of *Lippincott's Magazine*

In 1870, 485 of 2,265, or nearly one-fourth of Pueblo County residents, had migrated from New Mexico. This was the era of cattlemen, farmers, and merchants. One of eleven Puebloans was an immigrant. People we now identify as Germans gave their birthplace as being Hesse, Baden, Hanover, and other small principalities. Germany was not yet unified as one nation.

Pueblo merged into a city organization on March 26, 1873, when it appeared by the census that the population within the town limits had exceeded 3,000. The first city election was held on April 7, 1873. James Rice was elected as Pueblo's first mayor. G. P. Hayslip, O. H. P. Baxter, H. M. Morse, and Weldon Keeling were aldermen. Pueblo had boomed in 1872 due to the building of the railroad. Photograph courtesy of Pueblo Library District

Farming by Irrigation, Arkansas Valley, Near Pueblo, 1890s

Colorado's first water law, passed in 1876, (Article 16, Section 5 of the Colorado State Constitution), gave the right to others, as well as landowners, to use water. The State Engineer's Office, which controls irrigation, was established in 1879. In 1901 Colorado passed a law providing for the organization of irrigation districts. Photograph courtesy of the Pueblo Library District

Sheep Herd Near Pueblo

During the 1870s and 1880s, the wool industry in Colorado, Nebraska, Minnesota, Kansas, Wyoming, Utah, Idaho, and New Mexico grew. By 1884 it was a $50 million business based on 7.5 million sheep with an annual yield of 35 million pounds of wool. The tariff of 1867 in wool and woolens was reduced in 1883, and the wool industry declined. Photograph courtesy of the Pueblo Library District

Mahlon D. Thatcher (pictured with A. E. Reynolds on the right) and his brother John A. Thatcher were representative of the type of men who were able to make the transition from one economic era to the next. Mahlon came to Pueblo to join his brother John in general merchandising. John and Mahlon were from a Perry County, Pennsylvania, merchant family, and both had tried teaching. During the fifty years they were in business together, the brothers established a gigantic cattle business, bought large tracts of real estate, financed the first Pueblo smelter, invested in the beet sugar industry, encouraged the Atchison, Topeka and Santa Fe Railroad to come to Pueblo, and were leaders in the banking industry beginning in 1871 with the First National Bank of Pueblo. Photograph courtesy of the Pueblo Library District

Samuel C. Gallup, Circa 1890

Samuel Gallup was one of the early residents of Pueblo. He learned his trade from his brother Francis Gallup, who operated the famous Gallatin and Gallup Saddlery in Denver. The volunteer fire department and the city conventions were a part of Gallup's contribution to Pueblo. In 1880 Robert Frazier went to work in the Gallup shop and soon he was a partner. The name was changed to Gallup and Frazier.

The men had opposing views and personalities. After ten years the partnership ended. Gallup continued as S. C. Gallup until his death. Mrs. Gallup and their two sons continued the business until they sold it to James Wimmer and Karl Kretschmer. The S. C. Gallup Company closed in 1930. Photograph courtesy of the Pueblo Library District

Robert Frazier, Circa 1890

Robert Frazier was a more astute businessman than many saddlers and was the first to use advertising and slogans such as ''The world's largest manufacturer of cowboy saddles.'' His advertisements drew attention to Pueblo as ''the cowboy saddle capital.'' He had been at Pete Becker's saddle shop in Leadville and came to Pueblo to work for Samuel Gallup in 1880. Frazier died in the mid 1920s. Photograph courtesy of the Pueblo Library District

Pueblo Iron Horse Tree Saddle, From the 1896 S. C. Gallup and Frazier Catalog

During the peak of activity in the range cattle industry, there were three major saddlery houses located in Pueblo: the S. C. Gallup Company, the R. T. Frazier Saddlery, and the T. Flynn Saddlery. Thomas Flynn opened his shop in 1892. The 1921 flood wiped out the firm, which was located on Union Avenue, and Flynn died six months later. His son, Frank, took over the business and made a good recovery until the depression struck in 1929. Later Frank Flynn opened his own shop, the Boot and Saddle, in Carmel, California. Photograph courtesy of the Pueblo Library District

Pueblo Smelting and Refining Company

The four smelters operating in Pueblo in the 1890s were the Pueblo Smelting and Refining Company, the Colorado Smelting Company, the Philadelphia Smelting and Refining Company, and the Zinc Smelter. These smelters took the ores from the mines along the upper Arkansas River and melted the ore in order to separate the metal contained in the ore.

Mather and Geist built the first smelter in Pueblo in 1878 which was known as the

Pueblo Smelting and Refining Company. Smelter Hill and Goat Hill provided temporary housing for its immigrant employees. Anton Eilers was the general manager of the Colorado Smelting Company. Established in 1883-84, it was commonly known as the Eilers plant. It was located west of Santa Fe Avenue along the hill to Bessemer. Photograph courtesy of the Pueblo Library District

Chapter Three
Railroads and Smelters:
the Second Era

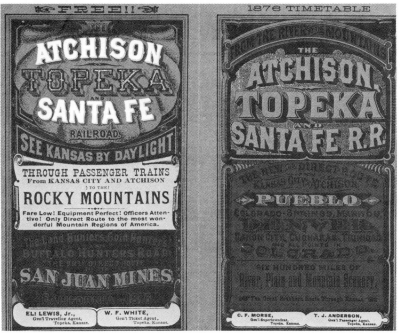

The Atchison, Topeka and Santa Fe Railroad Timetable Cover in 1876

The Atchison, Topeka and Santa Fe Railroad was the second railway to arrive in Pueblo. Next came the Denver and New Orleans Railroad, which was reorganized as the Denver, Texas and Gulf Railroad. The Missouri Pacific Railroad arrived in 1887, and the Rock Island Railroad commenced running cars to Pueblo in 1888. Timetable courtesy of the Pueblo Library District

Denver and Rio Grande Railroad, Circa 1890s

The efforts on the part of Pueblo citizens to bring the railroad industry to Pueblo created the second economic thrust of growth for the town. The railroads in turn encouraged the industrial growth of the community.

The first railroad to come to Pueblo was the Denver and Rio Grande, which had been organized in 1870 by General William J. Palmer. To prevent the railroad going to Canon City, the citizens voted on July 9, 1871, to issue $100,000 in bonds to support the extension of the Denver and Rio Grande narrow gauge to Pueblo. By June 1872 the track was brought into Pueblo. The terminal was in the southeast corner of a tract of land that later became part of Mineral Palace Park. On July 1, 1870, Congress had approved Gervacio Nolan's right to 48,695.48 of the 364,000 acres he claimed. By the time the Denver and Rio Grande was laying track toward Pueblo, the land had changed hands several times. The railroad purchased the portion of the land grant which bordered the Arkansas River and proceeded to plat its own rival town. Soon after the purchase the depot was moved to South Pueblo.

In June 1878 Pueblo County sued the Central Colorado Improvement Company for the return of the bond. The U.S. Supreme Court decided in the county's favor. Photograph courtesy of the Pueblo Library District

Union Avenue in 1870s

In a prospectus issued in 1874, two years after the railroad arrived in Pueblo, the Denver and Rio Grande Railway Company advertised the merits of their "Pueblo Colony" located in South Pueblo, Colorado. Under the guidance of the Central Colorado Improvement Company, people were encouraged to purchase certificates which entitled them to select lots or tracts of land within the colony. Inquiries could be sent either to the Central Colorado Improvement Company located in Pueblo or to the Denver and Rio Grande Railway Company in Pennsylvania. The railroad had organized the town of Colorado Springs and the Fountain Colony under the same system in 1871. The use of colonies was a part of the railroad's plan for the systematic development of the country along their route. South Pueblo

The efforts on the part of Pueblo citizens to bring the railroad industry to Pueblo created the second economic thrust for the town. By 1888 four major railroad lines from Pueblo were serving Colorado and bordering states. In search of business, the railroads encouraged the industrial growth of the community. Competition was strenuous and sometimes violent. Pueblo's location and the adjacent mineral deposits made it a practical location for the smelting industry. Soon Pueblo was known as the Smelting Capital of the World.

When the native population could no longer fill all of the needed jobs, immigrants were encouraged to come. Colorado's Bureau of Immigration promoted the state throughout the United States, and the smelters looked as far as Europe in search of new members for the labor force.

Pueblo's first neighborhoods were located adjacent to the work place. People walked to and from work, and long hours were spent on the job. Santa Fe Avenue was the first business district, followed by Union Avenue in South Pueblo. Goat Hill, Smelter Hill, and the Grove became homes for smelter workers. Steel workers lived in Bessemer, and the Blocks, located between the bluffs and Abriendo Avenue, became the home of railroad employees. Many of the prominent businessmen lived in the Blocks, while the most elaborate homes in the community were located near the Pueblo County Courthouse.

By the late nineteenth century Pueblo had become the second largest city in the state. The only barrier to continued growth was the lack of civic unity because of the existence of three towns—Pueblo, South Pueblo, and Central Pueblo—all located adjacent to one another.

was identified as a railroad, cattle, sheep, agriculture, mining, and manufacturing center, in that order.

John Edgar Thomson and Samuel M. Felton of Philadelphia and Louis H. Meyers of New York were the trustees for the colony's land.

The town of South Pueblo was incorporated October 27, 1873, and built of wooden buildings. Photograph courtesy of the Pueblo Library District

South Pueblo in 1879, the Denver and Rio Grande Railroad in the Foreground

Royal Gorge, Circa 1890

Palmer's forces were successful in regaining station after station. Pueblo, under the supervision of Bat Masterson, was the only holdout. Denver and Rio Grande Railroad forces considered stealing the cannon from the state armory but found that Bat had already appropriated it. The cannon was in the roundhouse with its muzzle trained on the attackers. R. F. Weitbree, a former Denver and Rio Grande engineer, talked to Bat Masterson under a protective truce. After a short discussion, Masterson ordered his men to surrender. Good sense or a bribe, either way the Royal Gorge war was over. Photograph courtesy of the Pueblo Library District

Between 1872 and 1888 Pueblo emerged as Colorado's railroad center. The access to the mining industries trade via the Royal Gorge was an important factor. The Royal Gorge war was fought by the Atchison, Topeka and Santa Fe Railroad and the Denver and Rio Grande Railroad over the right-of-way through the gorge to the boom town of Leadville, Colorado. For more than a year, while the legal battle was fought in court, violent conflicts were waged in the area of the gorge. Photograph courtesy of the Pueblo Library District

Bat Masterson

One of the memorable confrontations during the Royal Gorge war occurred in Pueblo. In 1879 Judge Thomas Bowen issued an order restoring the route to the Denver and Rio Grande Railroad, with instructions for sheriffs along the line to take possession at 6 a.m. on June 9. The Atchison, Topeka and Santa Fe Railroad hired Bat Masterson and sixty to sixty-five men from Dodge City, Kansas, to guard the roundhouse in Pueblo at any cost! Photograph courtesy of the Pueblo Library District

Colorado State Hospital's First Cottage, 1879

P. R. Thombs

Dr. P. R. Thombs, who was superintendent of the Colorado Insane Asylum from 1879 to 1899, stated his policies thus in his annual report for 1890:

The object of the Asylum treatment is the cure of the insane. I am not in favor of either over crowding or building large asylums . . . as such establishments serve principally for the custodial care of the inmates, and the Superintendent is compelled to devote a great share of his time to the business feature of the institution, thus interfering with the individualized care and treatment of the Patients.

An act to establish the Colorado Insane Asylum and providing for its location was approved February 8, 1879. Colorado Insane Asylum was opened October 23, 1879. The site contained a brick building that was remodeled, repaired, and opened for the reception of patients. At the same time this one-story frame cottage was erected for women.

Prior to the opening of the Colorado Insane Asylum the clerks of different counties sent the insane to Eastern asylums. By 1880 the capacity of the institution was thirty-eight. The first annual report revealed that seventy-seven patients had been admitted and twenty-five discharged. Photograph courtesy of the Pueblo Library District

Colorado Coal and Iron Co. Puebло. Col. A.H. Danforth Gen'l Mang'r

CASTING HOUSE.

CONVERTING WORKS.

Colorado Coal and Iron Company, Circa 1885

The general managers of the Colorado Coal and Iron Company were A. H. Danforth, 1880-88; T. Haskins Du Puy, 1888-89; John Dougherty, 1889-90; and Edward M. Steck, 1890-92.

The photograph is a line drawing of the steel works during the period that Danforth was manager. Photograph courtesy of the Pueblo Library District

Blast Furnace Betsy of the Colorado Coal and Iron Works, 1880

General William J. Palmer, founder of the CF&I Steel Corporation, was president of the three predecessor companies; the Central Colorado Improvement Company, established in 1872; the Southern Colorado Coal and Town Company, established in 1876; and the Colorado Coal and Steel Works Company, established in 1879. In 1880 the three companies were consolidated into the Colorado

Coal and Iron Company. Palmer continued as president until April 21, 1884. He was followed by Henry E. Sprague, 1884-89; Edward J. Berwind, 1889-92; and C. F. Meek, 1892.

The earliest known photograph of the

blast furnace "Betsy" is this one taken in 1880. Work on the furnace began February 2, 1880, and the furnace was blown in September 1881. Photograph courtesy of the CF&I Steel Corporation

Pueblo Union Depot

The Pueblo Union Depot is one of the finest railroad stations in Colorado. The depot, designed by Frank V. Newall of the Chicago firm of Sprague and Newall, was planned to accommodate heavy traffic. Built in 1889-90 under the supervision of James A. McGonigle, contractor, the depot originally served five railroads: the Denver and Rio Grande; Texas and Fort Worth; Chicago, Rock Island and Pacific; Atchison, Topeka and Santa Fe; and the Missouri Pacific. Photograph courtesy of the Pueblo Library District

Victoria Hotel, 1888

South Pueblo was laid out in three divisions. The first division, the bottom or low division bordering the Arkansas River, was intended for heavier branches of wholesale business and manufacturing interests. The railroad depot was located within this division. The second division, located along the upper or bluff portion, was titled Corona Park and skirted the west edge of the mesa to Abriendo Avenue. The winding streets formed irregular villa sites and occasionally groves of trees. This was to be the residential area. The third division was to be all of the land beyond Abriendo Avenue and was commonly known as the Blocks. The use of this land had not been determined.

A street passenger railroad that was to run down El Paso Avenue to Fifth Street was proposed. All of the streets in the

second and third divisions had Spanish names. Some of them were Valverde, Cristobal, Queretaro, Chihuahua, Guadalajara, and Zotula. During the period of consolidation most of the Spanish street names were changed, and only

Abriendo, Colorado, and Corona survived. Victoria Hotel stood on the northwest corner of B Street and Victoria Avenue across from the Union Depot. Photograph courtesy of the Pueblo Library District

52

Philadelphia Smelting and Refining Company

The Philadelphia Smelting and Refining Company, built in 1888, was the property of the Guggenheim family. Located adjacent to the Colorado Fuel and Iron Company, the smelter provided boarding-house accommodations for its employees in the community known as Harlem. Today the CF&I Steel Corporation's Pueblo plant encompasses its 100-acre site.

In 1899 a national smelter trust was formed, the American Smelting and Refining Company. By 1901 the Guggenheim family dominated the trust. As new methods for reducing ore were developed, the older plants were closed. Operation of the Philadelphia Smelter was discontinued in 1907; the Eilers in 1917; and the Pueblo smelter closed after the 1921 flood. The zinc smelter, operated by the U.S. Zinc Company, operated from 1893 to 1921. The community of Blende developed as a result of the zinc smelter. Photograph courtesy of the Pueblo Library District

Chinese Laundry Located on Santa Fe Avenue, 1880s

The 1880 census was the first that listed Chinese in Pueblo County. Seven Chinese men were employed as laundrymen and most of their shops were along Santa Fe Avenue. Several of the men lived together in a boardinghouse.

All five clerics of the Catholic Church listed in the 1880 United States census were immigrants. Three of the priests came from Italy and one from Ireland. The nun responsible for the Loretto Academy, a school, was from Ireland.

The population had tripled to 7,607. One of nine Puebloans was an immigrant. The population of 222 Germans was the largest immigrant group, followed by 202 Irish and 123 English. The Hispanic population was decreasing. Photograph courtesy of the Pueblo Library District

THE BURROS.

South Pueblo's first city hall was located on C Street between Main and Union streets. Incorporated October 27, 1873, the town was under trusteeship from 1873 to 1879. Stephen Walley was elected mayor in 1880 and 1881. Klaas Wildeboor was elected and served from 1882 to 1883. J. K. Shireman was elected mayor in 1884, and P. F. Sharp was elected in 1885.

In 1886 the town was consolidated with Pueblo and Central Pueblo. Photograph courtesy of the Pueblo Library District

South Pueblo's First City Hall Building

The Arkansas River and the Riverside Block, 1890s

The third Pueblo community, Central Pueblo, located along the eastern bank of the river, had been incorporated as a town on June 21, 1882. It must not have been a major event, because a careful check of the Daily Chieftain revealed no reference to the new community.

It was located on a small portion of the flood plain of the Arkansas River, on the left side of the photograph, where city hall and the health department are now located.

The smallness of Central Pueblo created some problems. One example is the candidate for city council who "ate and had his washing done in Central Pueblo, but did not sleep there regularly."

The first mayor who can be located for Central Pueblo was O. G. Chase. One of the organizers of the community, Dr. Cyrus F. Taylor, was the next mayor in 1884. Henry Rupps, elected mayor in 1885, was Central Pueblo's last mayor, due to consolidation.

Thus ended the four-year life span of Central Pueblo, the town that had been created between the towns of Pueblo and South Pueblo to avoid taxation. Photograph courtesy of the Pueblo Library District

54

Old Monarch, or the Hanging Tree, was located in the middle of Union Avenue in front of the present 218 South Union and about 150 feet north of C Street. The tree was twenty-nine feet in circumference and eighty-eight feet tall. This photograph was taken shortly before the tree was cut down on June 25, 1883. A group of citizens led by D. Holden tried to prevent the loss of the tree by gathering petitions to present to city council. The South Pueblo City Council learned of the petitions and adjourned early before the citizens could submit their petitions. The tree was cut down the next day. The story of the fourteen hangings from the tree is probably inaccurate. It is true that a new city council was elected at the next opportunity. Photograph courtesy of the Pueblo Library District

Old Monarch or the Hanging Tree, Circa 1880

Sacred Heart Cathedral

The Pueblo parish of the Catholic Church was established in June 1872. Father Charles M. Pinto, S. J., was the first parish priest. An Italian by birth, Father Pinto led the drive to build a church in 1873 at the corner of West and Thirteenth streets dedicated to St. Ignatius of Loyola. At first, after the church was completed, Father Pinto lived in a portion of the church building. In November 1875 he was succeeded by Father Francis N. Gutitosi, S. J., who was also Italian. On October 11, 1882, a fire broke out in a shed used by the fathers as a kitchen. The rectory and St. Ignatius were completely destroyed. There was no insurance on the building. Funds were raised for a new church building at a new location. Photograph courtesy of the Pueblo Library District

St. Patrick's Church and School

One of the earliest centers of the Catholic Church in Pueblo, St. Patrick's began under the care of the Jesuit fathers, who served the parish until 1925. Reverend Daniel Haugh secured seven lots on the southeastern corner of San Pedro and Guadalajara avenues, known as Michigan and Routt avenues today. St. Patrick's was dedicated on December 2, 1883, by Bishop Joseph Machebeuf of Denver. This was the second Catholic parish in Pueblo.

With St. Patrick's as headquarters, the parishes of St. Francis Xavier and Mount Carmel were established. Photograph courtesy of the Pueblo Library District

Bishop Joseph P. Machebeuf

In August 1883 Bishop Machebeuf officiated in the blessing of the new St. Ignatius at the corner of Grand Avenue and Eleventh Street. On November 1, 1887, Father Joseph Marra, superior of the Jesuit Mission in New Mexico and Colorado, turned St. Ignatius to Bishop Machebeuf (shown here). This ended the history of St. Ignatius with the Jesuit order. St. Patrick remained in their care. When the present structure was built in 1912 the name was changed to Sacred Heart. In 1941, when Pueblo became a diocese, Sacred Heart Church became Sacred Heart Cathedral. Photograph courtesy of the Pueblo Library District

William J. Palmer

The economic fate of South Pueblo was in turmoil in 1884 as the Denver and Rio Grande Railroad and the Colorado Coal and Iron Company stockholders fought with each other for control of their respective businesses. General Palmer, who had started both businesses, was no longer associated with the railroad, but was the president of the CC&I Company. Both companies shared the same stockholders. There was a move by Mr. Lovejoy, president of the railroad, to replace the Palmer-Philadelphia board with officials identified with the railroad. During this period A. H. Danforth, general manager of Colorado Coal and Iron Company, disclosed that his firm furnished one-third of the freight tonnage of the Denver and Rio Grande Railroad. Photograph courtesy of the Pueblo Library District

Dr. Hubert Allen Black

The Pueblo County Medical Society was organized August 20, 1881, when sixteen Pueblo physicians joined to improve the quality of medical care in the county. One of the first items of business was the formation of a board of censors. Most of the physicians practicing in the state were non-diploma physicians who had served some type of preceptorship, but had little or no formal education. Dr. P. R. Thombs was elected president. During the first *year much attention was given to the treatment of typhoid fever, diphtheria, smallpox, and post-partum sepsis. Dr. Hubert Allen Black, a member of the society, is shown here ready for his rounds in 1899. Photograph courtesy of the Pueblo County Medical Society*

St. Mary Hospital in the Grove

The first St. Mary Hospital was a two-story frame building, previously used as a boardinghouse, located in the Grove. The Sisters of Charity rented it for seventy-five dollars a month. It opened July 31, 1882. Later, the sisters acquired a building site at Quincy Street and Grant Avenue. In 1883 the first unit of the new St. Mary Hospital was constructed. Because of the great need for more space, equipment was moved from the original building to the new structure even before the windows and doors were hung. Photograph courtesy of the Pueblo Library District

St. Mary Hospital at Quincy Street and Grant Avenue

Several additions were made to the Quincy Street hospital building shown here. In 1904 an adjacent hospital building was erected, which brought the bed capacity to 150. The porches on the north were used for tuberculosis patients.

During the first twenty-five years of its existence, the institution was attended by the Jesuit fathers from St. Patrick's Church. In 1907 Father LaFevre was appointed the first chaplain. Photograph courtesy of Pueblo Library District

Chapter Four
Consolidation and Boom

Telegraph and Telephone Lines Along Santa Fe Avenue (Looking South), Circa 1881

Just four short years after the invention of the telephone, the Pueblo office of the Colorado Telephone Company got its start. The year was 1880 and there were fifty customers. In 1884 a long-distance line was extended from Denver to Colorado Springs to Pueblo. Puebloans could then talk to people outside of Pueblo. By the early 1900s telephone lines ran to most points in Colorado. Photograph courtesy of Pueblo Library District.

An early Pueblo City Council, Names Unknown

*T*his photograph of Pueblo's city council was taken when there were still nine members. The following is a list of Pueblo's mayors: James Rice (1873-75), John R. Lowther (1876), Mahlon D. Thatcher (1877), Weldon Keeling (1878), William H. Hyde (1879-80), George Q. Richmond (1881), John H. Warnecke (1882-84), T. G. McCarthy (1885), Delos Holden (1886), Charles Henkel (1887), Andrew Royal (1888), A. A. Grome (1889), Charles Henkel (1890), W. B. Hamilton (1891-92), Lewis B. Strait (1893-94), A. T. King (1895-97), James B. Orman (1897-99) and, George F. West (1899-1901). Mayor West died in office December 30, 1901. J. E. Rizer was appointed to serve from January 2 to July 21, 1902. He was followed by Benjamin B. Brown (1902-05), John T. West (1905-09), Abraham Lincoln Fugard (1909-11), and John T. West (1911). Photograph courtesy of the Pueblo Library District

Eighteen eighty-six saw the consolidation of the three Pueblos. A *Chieftain* newspaper article summed up the local sentiment by stating that while support for consolidation was "not as wide as a river nor as deep as a well," it would do. For most citizens, consolidation represented prosperity.

Some saw the potential increase in real estate; others saw the second largest city in the state becoming the largest. When reviewing the selection of a new government, one sage declared that "men who will hold a penny so near their eyes that they cannot see a dollar in making needed improvements should be given back seats" in the new government.

The Denver and Rio Grande Railroad representatives opposed consolidation. In the fourth ward of Pueblo, enthusiasts were trying a little fraud. The poll book showed a registration of 426 names while a canvass of the ward indicated a total of only 270 legal voters. The Republican party, which was the majority party, published a resolution in the newspaper stating that this attempt at fraud was a No-No.

On March 9, 1886, the voters of South Pueblo, Central Pueblo, and Pueblo went to the polls. Voter turnout was light. The vote tally read: in Pueblo, 788 for consolidation, 5 against; in Central Pueblo, 134 for 2 against; and in South Pueblo, 459 for and 80 against. The total vote was 1,381 for and 87 against.

From March 9 to April 6, 1886, Pueblo had three mayors: Henry Rupps from Central Pueblo, T. G. McCarthy from Pueblo, and P. F. Sharp from South Pueblo. On April 6, the Citizen's Consolidation Ticket and the Republican City Ticket competed for the new government positions. The Republican Ticket succeeded in electing the new mayor, Delos Holden, the new treasurer, A. E. Graham, and nine of the fourteen aldermen.

Bessemer Park, Circa 1903

The town of Bessemer was incorporated July 15, 1886, the same year Pueblo, South Pueblo, and Central Pueblo consolidated. Named for Henry Bessemer, developer of an inexpensive steel-making process, the community was annexed by the other Pueblos in 1894.

Bessemer's mayors were: Reese James *(1888), L. J. Taylor (1889), H. M. Sharp (1890), F. P. Hawke (1891), Dr. W. I. Shockey (1892), and J. K. Dempsey (1893).*

Bessemer Park appears here in the early 1900s. Photograph courtesy of the Pueblo Library District

Pueblo's Police Force, 1898

*B*efore consolidation each community had its own police force. In 1886, the year of consolidation, Pueblo's marshal was *Jack Gillen*, South Pueblo's marshal was *Jack Connor*, and Central Pueblo's peace officer was George Smith. In April, after the elections, H. P. Wooten was appointed chief of the new department. It was the responsibility of the mayor to appoint the chief of police. Thus, each new election saw the potential change of chief of police. Photograph courtesy of the Public Library District

Pueblo Police Force, 1911

*S*ome of Pueblo's police chiefs have been W. H. Haskell (1887-90); Jack Connor (1890); Charles O'Connor (1891-93); S. A. Abbey (1893-94); Joseph Loor (1895-96); Bob Griffin (1897-1902); W. F. McCafferty (1902); Dr. H. M. Shoop (1902-05); W. F. McCafferty (1905-1909); Don Sullivan (1909-?); Charles Yund (?-1911); and Denny McDermott (1911-?), Denny McDermott, the seventh person from the left in the center row, was appointed police chief after the commission form of government was adopted in 1911. Photograph courtesy of the Pueblo Library District

Board of Trade Building, Circa 1890

*T*he first association in the nature of a chamber of commerce was formed on January 20, 1869, under the name the Board of Trade of Southern Colorado. M. D. Thatcher was president. The principal work of this first organization was to gather statistics and advertise the advantages which southern Colorado offered to immigrants. On December 31, 1873, a second board of trade was organized under the title Board of Trade of Pueblo County. This board was instrumental in promoting the extension of the Santa Fe Railroad to Pueblo.

On June 14, 1882, the Board of Trade of the Pueblos was incorporated for the general promotion of trade in the three Pueblos—Pueblo, South Pueblo, and Central Pueblo. During this period, the Colorado Smelting Company and Missouri Pacific Railroad was established in Pueblo. Through its own action, a reorganization of this board was effected January 10, 1888, making it a stock company with capital stock at $50,000 in shares of $100 each. The membership fee was placed at $100, upon the payment of which the members received a full paid certificate of stock in the association. In 1890 the association erected its own building. The illustration shows the Board of Trade Building on the corner of Union Avenue and Richmond Street. On the first floor was the Pueblo Savings Bank, known today as the Pueblo Bank and Trust. Photograph courtesy of the Pueblo Library District

Puebloans Ready For a Railroad Excursion

*T*he active promotion of Pueblo by its citizens was a key factor in the development of the community. Creative, dynamic businessmen began to promote Pueblo in the 1880s. Known as "boosters," they were the most important factor in the emergence of Pueblo as the second largest city in Colorado. One aspect of boosterism was railroad excursion trips which encouraged people to go and see the wonders of Colorado. Photograph courtesy of the Pueblo Library District

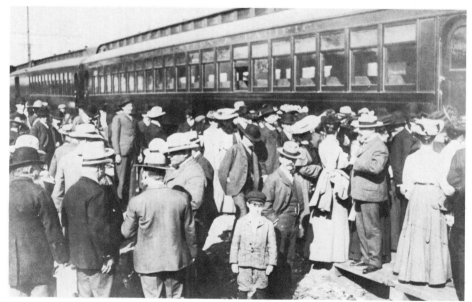

**F. H. Stewart and Company,
Circa 1890**

*F. H.Stewart and Company, located
on Union and Victoria avenues, began
as a blacksmith shop in 1876. In 1882
F. H. Stewart joined forces with his
brother A. T. Stewart. The specialty of
the firm was the manufacture of fine road*
*wagons, victorias, and carts. They carried
and manufactured a fine line of buggies
and wagons, agricultural equipment of all
kinds, and wagon and buggy harnesses.
Photograph courtesy of the Pueblo Library
District*

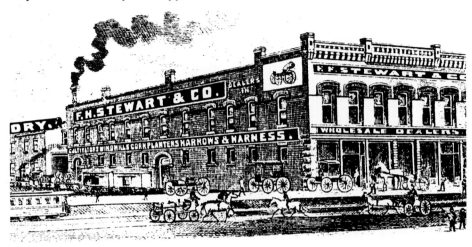

Charlie Carleton's Store

*By 1880, of every sixty people in Pueblo
one was a working woman. Women were
domestic servants, dressmakers, boardinghouse proprietors, and washerwomen.
Only four women were schoolteachers,
and women were not cooks. Men were
cooks. The clerks, such as those at Charlie
Carleton's store on Third Street, were
men. Photograph courtesy of the Pueblo
Library District*

Two Swearingen Brothers in the Family Water Barrel

In 1864 residents of Pueblo purchased water in barrels at the cost of twenty-five cents per barrel. The first Pueblo water system was started in 1874 when the population was about 3,000. By 1885 the area population was 26,000. In that year a private water company started a water system with treatment facilities located on the south side of the river. In 1906 the private system was purchased by the Southside Water District. The north side facility, or Gardner plant, served the area north of the Arkansas River, or District No. 2. Each district operated independently until 1957, when the two districts were consolidated by a vote of the citizens, forming the existing Board of Water Works of Pueblo. Photograph courtesy of the Swearingen family

Central High School, 431 East Pitkin Avenue

Pueblo School District 20 was the site of one of the earliest attempts at individualized instruction in the United States. Although Pueblo, South Pueblo, and Central Pueblo had consolidated, School District 20 remained a separate unit. Known as the Pueblo Plan, the program included guest lecturers (such as Dr. Richard W. Corwin), free textbooks, a student savings plan (proposed by Alva Adams), and the acknowledgment that individuals learn at different rates. Superintendent Preston W. Search supervised the program from 1888 to 1894 at Central High School, 431 East Pitkin Avenue. He wished the school district to be known as the Pueblo Industrial Schools and for industrial education to be given prominence in the program from kindergarten on.

South Pueblo was the home of many of the employees of the Colorado Coal and Iron Company and the various smelters.

Many of the students were the children of immigrants. English was frequently a second language for the kindergartener. Search's plan seemed suited to the needs of the community. At first it was well received; however, budget excesses created problems, and Search moved on to other schools. Photograph by John E. Smith

Clark Magnetic Mineral Spring Sanitarium, Circa 1905

The Clark Spring Water Company began in 1879 as the Pioneer Oil Company. In what was then South Pueblo, Silas Clark struck water at a depth of 1,425 feet on December 20, 1879, and one of Pueblo's oldest family businesses was begun. By January, Silas had determined that the artesian water was "very valuable for its medicinal qualities." A bathhouse was constructed, then a boardinghouse, so that those who wished to "take the cure" could be near the water.

Any Puebloan could partake of the water free of charge by coming to the well, but a charge of five cents a gallon was made for all that was taken away. By 1905 a fifty-seven-room sanitarium under the supervision of Dr. Louisa R. Black had been completed. Room and board for one week began at ten dollars. As part of the treatment patients drank twelve to sixteen glasses of water daily. Massage and vibrator treatments were also available. From the family ranch along Apache Creek south of Pueblo, fresh milk, cream, eggs, and butter were shipped daily by train.

In 1917 a group of doctors purchased the mineral spring property and prospered until the flood of 1921. Within a few years the property returned to the family. During the Depression water sales were traded for chickens, turkeys, eggs, and other items. At one point the sanitarium was sold for taxes to Arthur and Allen, General Contractors, for a bid of twenty-five dollars at a public sale. After struggling to repurchase the property, the family purchased the well from them for $2,500, and the family business returned to the selling of artesian water. Photograph courtesy of the Pueblo Library District

Early Pueblo Funeral Along Santa Fe Avenue

In the 1880s, when distinguished persons died, many businesses would close for burial rites. It was customary for a sixteen-piece band to play dirges at the head of the cortege as it passed through the business district. Black horses pulled black hearses for adults. White animals pulled white hearses for children. At the Arkansas River musicians would board surreys and ride to Riverview Cemetery, now Roselawn. At the entrance the bandsmen resumed marching and playing songs of mourning. The photograph was taken from Fourth Street looking north on Santa Fe Avenue. Photograph courtesy of the Pueblo Library District

American National Bank

Pueblo County Jail

Banks and banking have played a more important role in the development of Pueblo than is generally acknowledged. The Western National Bank, charted August 2, 1881, was started to provide banking facilities for the residents of South Pueblo and was closely associated with the steel works. Passbooks were balanced monthly, and all checks and deposits were entered by hand in the daily journal.

The American National Bank, charted August 31, 1889, was the first Pueblo Bank to provide safety deposit vaults. Some of the men associated with the bank were O. H. P. Baxter (president), Charles E. Gast (vice-president), and directors Benjamin Guggenheim, Frank Pryor, Charles Henkel, and T. G. McCarthy. The Minnequa Bank of Pueblo, incorporated March 4, 1902, with M. D. Thatcher, G. W. Bowen, and Fred C. Roof as directors, had an extensive foreign exchange trade. Area immigrants used the bank to send money home. Photograph courtesy of the Pueblo Library District

The Pueblo County Jail shown here was a rotary jail. Patented on July 12, 1881, the portion of jail seen on the right provided a kitchen for the prisoners, office space, and individual cells for women and juveniles. In a separate unit, on the left of the building, was the rotary unit and cage. This consisted of a giant gridded, stationary, cylindrical enclosure or cage bolted to the floor and ceiling. Inside the outer gridded drum was an inner rotary cylinder divided into two levels, or decks, each segmented into ten pie-shaped cells. The inner cylinder was constructed around a central axis which rested on bearings at the base. There was one door at each level in the outer shell. Each cell in the inner drum had a doorway but not door.

Entrance was gained to respective cells by rotating the inner cylinder opposite the single door in the outer stationary cylinder. Each cell was made of iron plate and contained double bunk beds. At the apex of the cell was a recessed toilet. Each cell was eight feet high and seven-and-a-half feet to the center. The jail design was hazardous for the prisoners. Bones were broken by having arms, hands, or legs caught between the bars during the revolving of the cylinder. Photograph courtesy of the Pueblo Library District

Doyle Cemetery With the White House in the Background, Circa 1921

Early Colorado statutes allowed any three individuals the right to create a cemetery. Family cemeteries on the home ranch were a common occurrence. Some of the cemeteries in Pueblo County are Northside Cemetery, Roselawn Cemetery (originally known as Riverside), Chico Cemetery, Doyle Cemetery, which is seen here, St. Vrain Cemetery, Mountain View Cemetery, and Imperial Memorial Gardens.

Some of the lost cemeteries include the Pest House Cemetery and the Colorado State Hospital Cemetery. The Pest House was located north of town and was used for persons with communicable diseases such as small pox.

All deaths occurring between June 1, 1884, and May 1885 were recorded in the state census. Causes of death were small-pox, cholera, liver disorders, mountain fever, poisoning, and consumption. One industrial death was reported, a railroad accident. Photograph courtesy of the Pueblo Library District

Tabor Lutheran Church

A state census was conducted in 1885. In the five years since 1880 Pueblo's population had again doubled, to 16,026. Arapahoe, Lake, and Pueblo counties were the three most populated counties. The largest immigration group was Irish, followed by Germans and English. A significant increase in the number of northern Europeans from Sweden, Den-mark, and Finland occurred during this period. Two Swedish communities developed. One was in the Elm Street and Northern Avenue area and the other in the Abriendo Avenue and Tyler Street area. The Tabor Lutheran Church at 115 West Fourth Street was sponsored by the Swedish community. Photograph courtesy of the Pueblo Library District

First Methodist Church Circa 1880

The first Methodist meeting in the Pueblo area was a camp meeting held under the huge cottonwood tree known as the Hanging Tree or Old Monarch. Reverend William Hobert, a circuit rider, is credited with serving Pueblo at that time. In 1866 the first regular Methodist church organization was affected with E. H. Kirkbride as pastor.

In 1869 an adobe church was built at Seventh and Main streets. It served the congregation until 1884. In that year, a new brick structure was built at Ninth and Main streets.

First Methodist Church, Now First United Methodist Church

On January 1, 1923, ground was broken at Eleventh and Court streets for the present church structure. The church at Ninth and Main streets became the property of the Salvation Army. Later the First Methodist Church joined with the United Bretheran Church to become the First United Methodist Church.

The Methodist Conference sponsored the Spanish-language newspaper Hermidad, *which was edited by Alexander Darley and published in Pueblo. The first published accounts of* pentitentes *appeared in this newspaper. Photograph courtesy of John Suhay*

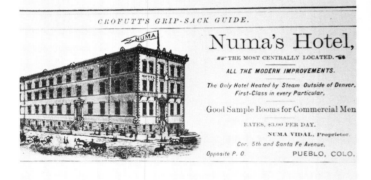

J. D. Miller's Groceries and Crockery

The Colorado state census for 1885 recorded Pueblo's population at 16,026. The Chieftain *cost twenty-five cents or one dollar a month—the paper was still a weekly. At Delmonico's restaurant at 198 Union Avenue the regular meal was twenty-five cents, and meat orders served at the counter cost fifteen cents. Marathon roller skating at DeRemer's was the newest rage. If one wasn't feeling too well, Mustang Liniment was advertised for use by man and beast.*

J. D. Miller's grocery store sold crockery as well as fruits and produce. Photograph courtesy of the Public Library District

The Original Grand Hotel Building, Circa 1888

The Grand Hotel opened on September 3, 1887. Four stories high, the Grand with its rotunda, lavish parlors, reception rooms, and 100 "chambers" was in the tradition of lavish nineteenth-century Colorado hotels. An early Pueblo journalist bragged, "The Grand is the only hotel on this continent where the top floor is furnished in the same style as the second." The billiard room and bar on the first floor was thought by many to be the most magnificent bar in Colorado. N. W. Clemons, the presiding genius, had insisted that the Grand be a Pueblo hotel, built with Pueblo capital, and owned by Pueblo men. It was furnished by local merchants with many of the items especially manufactured for the hotel. Photograph courtesy of the Pueblo Library District

Hotel Numa

The building currently used by the Benevolent and Protective Order of Elks, located on the corner of Fifth Street and Santa Fe Avenue, began as the Hotel Numa. Photograph courtesy of the Pueblo Library District

The Congress Hotel, Formerly Known as the Grand Hotel

In 1910 the name of the Grand Hotel was changed to the Congress in honor of the National Irrigation Congress, whose 1910 convention was held in Pueblo. The Spanish mission style portion of the hotel was added at that time. Photograph courtesy of the Pueblo Library District

Principal Features of the City

The May 12, 1888, issue of Harper's Weekly *identified as the principal features of the community (1) the Santa Fe Avenue business district, (2) the Arkansas River, (3) the exhibit of a portion of Old Monarch which depicted the age of the tree, (4) the Colorado Insane Asylum, (5) an adobe home built by "Mexicans," and (6) the Central High School. Photograph courtesy of the Pueblo Library District*

The Fariss Hotel, 315 North Union Avenue, Circa 1890

The Fariss Hotel, J. R. Fariss, proprietor, offered the following amenities in the 1890s: 100 rooms, artesian bathhouse, mineral well for drinking water, and electric streetcars that passed every five minutes. Photograph courtesy of the Pueblo Library District

Arkansas Valley Railway Light and Power Company Trolley Car

The Pueblo City Railway Company by 1891 had twenty-five miles of track, five separate lines, and operated from 6:00 a.m. to midnight. The combined daily travel was over 3,000 miles. Photograph courtesy of the Pueblo Library District

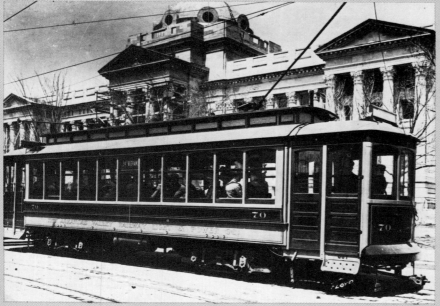

Young Pueblo Girls

*T*he 1887 attempt by the Ladies' Benevolent Union to obtain state funds for their home for homeless girls and women failed. A religious, charitable organization, the Union, located on the corner of Third and D streets, had been organized for five years and owned its own building and grounds. By 1890 the program included free employment service for women, a home for children, nursing care, temporary shelter, meals for transients, charity funerals, and free clothing. Photograph courtesy of Gladys Hassey

Guggenheim Building's Frieze

A rough estimate based only on women in the city in 1890 shows that 37 percent were widows. Usually they had no visible means of support.

In the period from 1870 to 1900, one prostitute was listed by occupation in the federal population census. The illegal nature of the profession led its practitioners to be a bit elusive when the census taker visited. The state hospital officials were also at a loss to identify the occupations of some female patients. On one report they listed "sporting lady." All other reports made no reference to prostitution.

This was the period when the Guggenheim family was deeply involved in the smelting business in Pueblo. Several of the sons were residing here. Ben Guggenheim was chief of staff of the Philadelphia Smelting and Refining Company and frequently entertained the town's residents as his surrey headed for the "row." He even visited the opera house with the madam herself, who, bedizened in his diamonds, blew kisses in all directions to her many friends—customers.

Pictured here is the name of the Guggenheim Building on Main and Fourth streets. The first two floors were built in 1897, and the last two floors were added in 1902.

The Guggenheim Building was razed in 1982. Photograph courtesy of the Public Library District

A View of Pueblo From the Mesa, 1888

Judge Andrew Royal was elected mayor of Pueblo in 1888. His biography reads like a Horatio Alger story come true.

Andrew Royal was born in Kingsdale, County Cork, Ireland, in 1836. During the famine year of 1848, when he was eleven, his widowed mother came to America. In April of that year they landed in New York. It was there that Andrew wandered away from the hotel and, being unable to find his way back, was picked up by a policeman. When asked his name, he said ''Riehill,'' which was mistaken at police headquarters for Royal. The misspelling of the name prevented his mother from finding him, and after a lengthy period of investigation the lost boy was finally adopted by a Quaker family named Butterworth, who lived at Mount Holly, New Jersey.

Andrew lived with the Butterworth family until he was sixteen. Then he traveled to Toledo, Ohio, then to Chicago, Illinois, and eventually to Maryville,

Missouri. There he studied law and was admitted to the bar. During the Civil War he enlisted in the Union army on the first call of President Lincoln for three years' service, and subsequently reenlisted and served through the five years of the war. His army record shows that he was in thirty battles and about forty long marches. He was mustered out at the end of his service as a captain. In 1859 he married Hester Markham, and to this union six chldren were born. Four of the children died in early childhood.

Andrew Royal came to Pueblo in 1881 from Maryville, Missouri, where he had been a member of the law firm of Anthony, Royal, and Morehouse. In Missouri he had served as probate judge and had since been called Judge Royal. Soon after coming to Pueblo, Judge Royal purchased the **Weekly Democrat** *and started the first evening newspaper published in Pueblo. For many years he was the proprietor of the Southern Hotel, on*

Victoria Avenue, later known as the Royal Hotel. His career in politics included serving Pueblo County in the state legislature in 1882 and 1883, and as mayor in 1888. During his term as mayor he did much to improve the city. The parks on the mesa were planned and improved. Royal Park, which was named after him, was graded down from an unsightly hill, and most of the trees were planted by his own hand. Today the Pueblo Library District is located in the park.

In 1885 Andrew Royal made a trip to Ireland, where he learned his correct family name and that his mother and sister were still in the United Staes. For Puebloans he represents the first immigrant to become mayor of Pueblo.

The illustration is of Pueblo in 1888, the year Judge Royal was mayor. Photograph courtesy of the Pueblo Library District

Consolidated Pueblo's First City Hall, 1889

The year 1889 found Pueblo struggling with the problem of becoming one community. Following consolidation the city did not know what its indebtedness was. The city clerk insisted that the books be "put into shape!"

The most significant activity in Pueblo was the construction industry. In a special article on March 17, 1889, the Colorado Daily Chieftain *documented that 269 buildings were currently under construction.*

City council had accepted the new city hall, shown here, from the contractor, Mr. Crowell, on March 12, 1889.

The minutes before the council for their first meeting in the new chambers included a petition from an angry citizen regarding boys setting fire to his outhouse. Photograph courtesy of the Pueblo Library District

The Rood Candy Company, Circa 1900

The Rood Candy Company, 406 West Seventh Street, was an important employer of women. By the 1890s job specialization had begun. Black women were called washerwomen, while white wmen doing the same work were called laundresses. Boardinghouses were giving way to furnished rooms. Dressmakers were supplemented by tailoresses and seam- *stresses. Women began to be employed as clerks and salesladies.*

By 1900 women were employed in positions that were to become stereotyped as women's jobs. They were telephone operators, teachers, and stenographers. Photograph courtesy of the Pueblo Library District

The Fountain Lake Hotel, built in 1889, was a part of the Pueblo real estate boom. The anticipated support for the hotel and housing plan did not materialize. For a time the owners were offering the site to the newly formed Pueblo Country Club for one dollar a year. The artificial lake created adjacent to the hotel dried up, and the hotel was generally abandoned. During prohibition, 1916 to 1933, it became a roadhouse and speakeasy. The building burned in 1926. Today, the outline of where the building once stood can be found on the slope west of the University of Southern Colorado before one reaches University Park. Photograph courtesy of the Pueblo Library District

Thurlow-Hutton Central Block Building

The Thurlow-Hutton Central Block was built on the southeast corner of Second and Main streets in 1889 of red Manitou sandstone. The center was an open rotunda from the first to fifth floor. When it caught fire one night in August 1953, it was an inferno that could not be controlled. O. G. Pope, an attorney, was alseep in his office and burned to death. Photograph courtesy of the Pueblo Library District

Rocky Mountain Oil Company
Refinery at Eden, Circa 1890

The discovery of the Florence oil field and subsequent oil drilling created a new market—oil refining. In July 1891 a section of land north of Pueblo was purchased by the Z. V. Trine Investment Company. Realtor Andre J. Overton was the treasurer. Sixty acres were sold to the Rocky Mountain Oil Company and the remainder divided into the Overton plat.

By September 1891 construction had begun on the buildings, furnaces, and a pipeline from Florence. By February 1892 the refinery was ready. The pump at Florence was started, but nothing came out at Overton. A larger pump was installed and the pipeline was cleared of rabbit carcasses and other debris. Complicated economic issues caused the refinery to be deeply in debt by January 1893. In 1894 floods damaged the railroad facilities and soon the oil refinery was closed. Photograph courtesy of the Pueblo Library District

The Colorado Coal and Iron
Company, 1888

In 1892 the Colorado Coal and Iron Company consolidated with its rival, the Colorado Fuel Company, to form the Colorado Fuel and Iron Company. The prime of the merger was John C. Osgood, who assumed the office of president. Osgood served from 1892 to 1900. He was followed by J. A. Kebler, 1900-03; F. J. Hearne, 1903-06; J. F. Welborn, 1906-29; and Arthur Roeder, 1929-38. The company appears here in 1888. Photograph courtesy of the Pueblo Library District

Colorado Fuel and Iron Company,
Pueblo Steel Works, 1901

The general superintendents of the steel works have been Daniel N. Jones, 1881-88; Rees James, 1888; J. B. Nau, 1888-89; S.S. Murphy, 1890; Independence Grove, 1891-92; T. W. Robinson, 1892-1901; C. S. Robinson, 1901-06; J. B. McKennan, 1906-15; Frank Parks, 1915-24; H. B. Carpenter, 1924-28; L. F. Quigg, 1928-46; A. F. Franz, 1946; and J. J. Martin, 1946. The blast furnace is shown here on July 24, 1901. Photograph courtesy of the Pueblo Library District

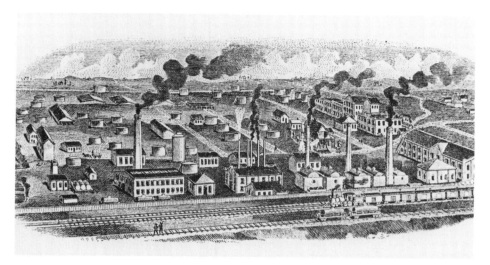

**The Mahlon D. Thatcher Home,
Razed in 1976**

The Mahlon D. Thatcher home occupied a hill bordered by Fifteenth, Elizabeth, Sixteenth, and Greenwood streets. During and following World War II, it was used as an American Red Cross chapter house. The Red Cross sold it to the Southern Colorado Consistory.

A small housing development can be seen in the right rear portion of the photograph. Following the consolidation of the three Pueblos, real estate boomed. Irregular patterns of housing construction occurred. It was not until the 1950s that the area platted in the late 1880s was actually filled with housing. Photograph courtesy of John Suhay

The First Presbyterian Church in Pueblo

Under the jurisdiction of the presbytery in Denver, Reverend Sheldon Jackson arrived in Pueblo in 1870. Upon making a house-to-house canvass, he found one Baptist, eleven Methodist, four Episcopalians, four Roman Catholics (not including Mexicans), two United Brethren, three Lutherans, two Jews, four Congregationalists, and four Presbyterians.

Presbyterian church services were begun in the first courthouse. The second site of worship was Centennial School. From there the congregation moved to the second courthouse on Tenth Street between Main and Court streets. In November 1872 the congregation purchased lots at Ninth and Court streets, and the first Presbyterian church in Pueblo was built. These lots and the church building were later sold. Photograph courtesy of the Pueblo Library District

Pueblo Metropolitan Museum, Circa 1900

Rosemount, John A. Thatcher's residence at 419 West Fourteenth Street, was built between 1891 and 1893. Holly and Jelliff of New York were the architects. The house is faced with rose lava stone. Today, the Pueblo Metropolitan Museum operates the home as an example of a Victorian house. Photograph courtesy of John Suhay

First Presbyterian Church, Built in 1890

On September 7, 1890, the second church building at Tenth and Court streets was dedicated. Beautiful Tiffany windows illuminate the sanctuary. Photograph courtesy of John Suhay

81

Penitente Service, Circa 1893

*O*n the plains and in the valleys of southern Colorado and New Mexico, Hispanic laymen have gathered for generations to worship. Their religious organization is known as **La Hermandad de Nuestros Padre Jesus** *or more commonly as the* **Penitentes.** *Illustration courtesy of the Pueblo Library District*

Alexander Darley, 1893

*T*he first accounts of the **Penitentes** *were published in Pueblo, Colorado, in April 1890 by Alexander Darley. His views on the* **Penitentes** *were published in the Presbyterian missionary Spanish-language newspaper* La Hermandad. *In 1893 Darley's reports and illustrations were published in a small book titled* **The Passionists of the Southwest, or the Holy Brotherhood.** *The book, published in Pueblo, was copyrighted in English and Spanish. Photograph courtesy of the Pueblo Library District*

First Congregational Church

*T*he first Congregational church was organized September 3, 1878. It was established as a part of the westward missionary movement of the Congregational churches. In 1889 the site at Evans Avenue and Jackson Street was purchased, and plans for the building were drawn. The new building included a stained-glass window from Tiffany in New York and was constructed of red sandstone. Formal dedication was held on February 13, 1890. Photograph courtesy of John Suhay

Parade on Union Avenue

Parades such as this one were used to advertise special events such as the circus. Photograph courtesy of Gladys Hassey

An Early Pueblo Hose Company

The volunteer fire departments were organized along democratic principles. Each April the members of the fire department met and elected a new chief and assistant chief. In early years, when membership was smaller, the election was a relatively simple affair. By 1888 there were 240 members with all but 13 present and voting. The balloting commenced shortly after 11:00 a.m. and continued until 10:00 p.m.

Some of the early volunteer fire chiefs were Samuel Gallup, 1879 and 1880; Benjamin F. Davis, 1882; Henry O. Morris, 1883; M. Lehman, 1886; Charles Otero, 1887; G. W. Gill, 1888; and R. J. Krague, 1889. Photograph courtesy of the Pueblo Library District

Robert J. Krague, Pueblo's First Paid Fire Chief

The City of Pueblo Fire Department was created by city council on July 16, 1889. The members of the new paid department were selected from the volunteer force. Robert J. Krague, shown here, was the first chief. His term in office ended with his death on July 31, 1891.

The funeral arrangements for Chief Krague reflect the political and social role of the fire department in the late nineteenth century. The initial notice of Chief Krague's death appeared on the bottom of the fourth page of the newspaper. Chief Krague died when he was thrown out of his buggy, pulled by Tom, his runaway horse.

As the plans for the funeral unfolded, the newspaper space allotted to the event grew. Following Chief Krague's death at St. Mary Hospital, he was taken to McMahon and Collier Funeral Home. Soon it was decided that he should lie in state at the city council chambers from 4:00 p.m. Saturday to 10:00 a.m. Sunday. The chambers and hallways were draped with black-and-white bunting with rosettes at the corners. Foliate plants and flowers in pots were placed on the nearby desks. Photograph courtesy of the Pueblo Library District

Pueblo Fire Department Hose Company No. 1 Ready for Chief Krague's Funeral

On Sunday the funeral service for Chief Robert J. Krague was held in his home at 315 West Ninth Street. Reverend R. S. Radcliff of Ascension Episcopal Church officiated. Following the service the funeral procession formed on Grand Avenue above Ninth Street. The assistant fire chief served as grand marshal in a procession nearly two miles in length. The route was east on Ninth Street to Santa Fe Avenue to Main Street to Union Avenue to C Street to lower Santa Fe Avenue and thence to Riverview Cemetery.

The procession began with Grand Marshal Sanborn and his aides, Chief of Police O'Connor and T. C. Cramer, followed by a platoon of police; the firemen's band; the members of the fire department with all of the apparatus draped in black-and-white bunting; Pueblo Lodge No. 90 B.P.O.E.; Stanchfield's band; A.O.U.W. lodges; Red Men Lodge; the mayor, aldermen, and city officers in carriages.

After the city officers marched delegations from the Denver, Colorado Springs, and Manitou fire departments. Next came the carriages reserved for the pallbearers, then the hearse, beside which marched the

pallbearers. The hearse was followed by the late chief's buggy drawn by Tom, the horse whose wildness had caused his death. Next to last was the carriage occupied by Mrs. Krague followed by a long line of carriages containing friends. Chief Krague's funeral was the most elaborate ever held in Pueblo. Photograph courtesy of the Pueblo Library District

Pueblo Fire Truck No. 1, Circa 1911

During the next two decades the chiefs of the fire department changed with regularity. Krague's assistant, T. D. Sanborn, was appointed chief and remained in office until April 7, 1892. He was followed by George W. Hook, who served until April 19, 1895. Hook was followed by Sam Herdy until April 19, 1897, when H. M. Shoup became chief and served until April 1899. It was obvious that during this time the position of fire chief was a political office, and the position changed with the municipal election.

Elmer Otterbine Ringer was the next chief, followed by P. D. McCartin, C. B. Willis, and Sam Christy. The frequent changes in leadership evidently did not effect the quality of Pueblo's fire prevention. By 1912 Pueblo was claiming the lowest fire loss per capita of any city in America. Photograph courtesy of the Pueblo Library District

Grand Opera House Entrance

In 1889 the Grand Opera House Association was formed and soon two of the finest architects in the country, Adler and Sullivan of Chicago, were hired to design the building. Louis Sullivan was the partner who undertook the design of the opera house. During the planning stage of the building, Sullivan wrote to Pueblo stating that "a building should be adapted to the climate of the locality in which it is built." Later he wrote that "every city should have an architecture distinctly its own." In harmony with this philosophy, the exterior of the opera house featured slabs of Manitou red rock and granite. The decorative effect was secured by means of elaborate stone carving. The seating capacity was 1,100, nearly that of the Tabor Grand Opera House in Denver. Photograph courtesy of the Pueblo Library District

Grand Opera House, Circa 1900

Located on Main and Fouth streets the Grand Opera House served Pueblo from September 9, 1890, to March 1, 1922. A virtual parade of eminent people spoke or performed on its stage, including such well known people as Theodore Roosevelt and the Russian ballerina Anna Pavlova. Photograph courtesy of the Pueblo Library District

86

First National Bank Interior

This interior view of the lobby of the First National Bank is the only known surviving interior photograph of the Grand Opera House. From 1890 to 1914 the bank occupied the entire corner of the first floor. Earlier (1871-90) the bank had been at the corner of Fourth Street and Santa Fe Avenue. Photograph courtesy of the Pueblo Library District

**Grand Opera House Fire
March 1, 1922**

The fire that destroyed the Grand Opera House building on March 1, 1922, broke out on a severe winter night. The fire was spotted at 1:15 a.m. in the dance hall, which was originally called a "summer garden," on the top floor. By 1:50 a.m. the roof had collapsed, and by 2:00 a.m. all floors of the building had fallen in. At one time the building had housed the First national Bank of Pueblo and sixty other businesses. Photograph courtesy of the Pueblo Library District

Colorado Mineral Palace Grounds

The Colorado Mineral Palace was first suggested by General Cameron, of Canon City, who probably received inspiration from the ice, corn, coal, and spring palaces recently erected in other areas. The purpose of the mineral palace was to advertise Colorado's mineral resources to the world. Photograph courtesy of the Pueblo Library District

Colorado Mineral Palace Sculptured Garden

Pueblo architect Otto Burlow's design for the building was accepted, although many changes occurred during construction. At one point there was a plan to have no windows, and for all light to be artificial. The building was 224 feet long and 134 feet wide. The construction cost was $165,000.

The Colorado Mineral Palace opened to the public July 4, 1891. Photograph courtesy of John Suhay

Ceiling of the Colorado Mineral Palace

Levy of New York designed the interior of the Colorado Mineral Palace. The ceiling was ninety feet high with twenty-eight domes. The center dome was ninety feet in diameter, two others forty-two feet each, and the remaining twenty-five domes twenty-eight feet. Each dome was decorated with Colorado wildflowers. The artist for the domes was an unknown Italian. In the center dome there were four medallions typifying stages of the state's growth. First was an Italian, followed by a prospector, a cowboy, and a merchant. Photograph courtesy of the Pueblo Library District

The Silver Queen and King Coal of the Colorado Mineral Palace

The Colorado Mineral Palace stage, built to accommodate an orchestra, represented a grotto constructed of stalactites and stalagmites. In the back was a mountain stream, a waterfall, and Pike's Peak. At intervals a miniature burro pack train loaded with a miner's outfit toiled up the steep. Originally there was to be a nymph grasping a sparkling mineral nugget and rising and falling in the stream.

King Coal and Silver Queen were located at the sides of the stage. Trinidad contributed King Coal to the palace in honor of their coal industry. Aspen contributed Silver Queen. In 1935 the Colorado Mineral Palace closed. Vandals stole the Silver Queen and King Coal bit by bit. When the building was razed, the only surviving portion of the figures was an arm of the Silver Queen. Photograph courtesy of John Suhay

Colorado Mineral Palace Hall

The original collection for the Colorado Mineral Palace consisted of the ores and specimens collected by the different counties of Colorado for the St. Louis World's Fair. The display cases were located at the bottom of the columns.

Some of the Colorado mineral specimens were wire gold from Breckenridge, pyrargyrite from Silverton, fluorite from Wagon Wheel Gap, geothite from El Paso County, and cerrusite from Leadville. Photograph courtesy of the Pueblo Library District

Colorado Mineral Palace in 1938

Over the years the wooden palace building with stone columns became worn, and in 1935 it closed. During the worst days of the Depression the minerals were sold. Paul H. Keating, under the WPA program, supervised the dispersement of the minerals. On July 27, 1938, three truckloads of minerals were sold to the American Smelting and Refining Company in Leadville. Approximately $800 was given to the city after all the expenditures had been made. The building was razed in 1942. Photograph courtesy of the Pueblo Library District

Colorado State Fair, Circa 1890s

In 1872 a group of Pueblo businessmen organized the Southern Colorado Agricultural and Industrial Association. The first show was held October 9, 1872, in the present Mineral Palace Park area, which the association had purchased for $3,000. Races were the most popular feature. A grandstand seating 500 with standing room for 500 more was erected. On October 11, 1872, attendance was reportedly 1,400.

The State Fair Association was incorporated in November 1886 and continued at the same location. The Colorado Mineral Palace is on the right side in the background. Photograph courtesy of John Suhay

Early Colorado State Fair Exhibit

In January 1890 the association purchased eighty acres west of Lake Minnequa from the Colorado Coal and Iron Company, and sold the fifty-acre original *tract to the Colorado Mineral Palace promoters. Photograph courtesy of John Suhay*

Joseph Hitchins

Joseph Hitchins (1838-93) was Pueblo's professional resident artist from the 1870s to his death in 1893. The son of an English art collector, Hitchens had the opportunity to study under Europe's great masters. He visited virtually all the major galleries in Europe and studied at the famed Dusseldorf School in Germany. Following his father's death, Hitchins went to Canada and lived in Montreal briefly before moving to Colorado. His Pueblo studio was at 322 Santa Fe Avenue and his home at 307 West Twelfth Street. Many young Pueblo women took lessons from him. Photograph courtesy of the Pueblo Library District

A Hitchins Painting

This nine-by-twelve-inch oil on board by Hitchins called Confluence of the Arkansas and Fountain Rivers *is a part of the Francis King Collection of the Sangre de Cristo Arts and Conference Center. Other examples of his work may be found at the Pueblo Metropolitan Museum and Denver Public Library's Western History Department.*

Hitchins was known for the atmosphere of his paintings, the blending of colors, and the selection of tones. Photograph courtesy of the Francis King Collection

Mount Pleasant Boardinghouse, Circa 1889

Alfred Damon Runyon, short story writer and columnist, grew up in Pueblo with his father, a typesetter. The entire family had moved to Colorado in 1887, when Alfred Damon was seven years old. Soon his mother and three sisters returned to Kansas. He and his father lived at several locations before settling at the Mount Pleasant Boardinghouse about 1891. Located on the corner of Summit, now called Albany, and Sixth streets, the boardinghouse provided easy access to the Santa Fe Avenue and Main Street area of Pueblo. Photograph courtesy of the Pueblo Library District

The *Chieftain* Newspaper Building

As a reporter, Runyon lived through and recorded the great social change that was to result in modern America. In many ways, Runyon's theme was the life of his times. According to his own estimate, he wrote 80 million words. As a boy hanging around outside the Chieftain office with his friends, his goal was to become an editor at one of the local newspapers. For a brief period, in 1900 and 1903, Runyon did work for the Chieftain before moving to Denver and then to New York.

In later years Damon Runyon told colorful stories of the years that he spent with his father. One of the stories he forgot was about how his father ran on the Populist Party ticket for city clerk in 1893. He lost, and perhaps that's why his son forgot. Photograph courtesy of John Suhay

Hinsdale School

In later years Damon Runyon told colorful stories of his youth in Pueblo. He liked to remember himself as "a bad little boy." Hinsdale School, shown here, was the school he attended irregularly. According to popular story he was expelled. His school records have been lost, so the truth of his education will never be known. However, he must have attended class occasionally, for his first newspaper job was with the Evening Post and by age fourteen he had his first assignment—a lynching! Photograph courtesy of John Suhay

Pueblo Soldiers in the Philippines, 1898

In 1898 Damon Runyon joined the Minnesota Volunteers, having been rejected in Pueblo because of his age, to participate in the Spanish-American War. In the Philippines he was able to spend time with the Pueblo boys and sent stories back to the Chieftain. *Photograph courtesy of the Pueblo Library District*

Union Avenue in the 1890s

The Home Cafe and the Bucket of Blood were the two saloons that Damon Runyon mentions as being his favorites. The Bucket of Blood was a notorious saloon located somewhere on Union Avenue, and the Home Cafe was on Main Street. The dates of the Home Cafe challenge Runyon's stories of his sinful youth, since it was not listed in the city directories until 1899. Runyon would have been eighteen when his favorite saloon opened. Photograph courtesy of the Pueblo Library District

Colorado Fuel and Iron Company Baseball Team

Baseball has probably been Pueblo's favorite sport. On January 20, 1910, during a trip to Pueblo, Damon Runyon was elected president of the Colorado State Baseball League. By the first week of April the league was declared defunct. Puebloans, such as the above Colorado Fuel and Iron Company team, continued to play baseball. Photograph courtesy of the Pueblo Library District

Alfred Damon Runyon, Circa 1905

By 1905 Alfred Damon Runyon (he wasn't to drop the Alfred until he moved to New York City) had begun his career in Denver. In 1905 he worked for the Denver Republican *and the the* Denver Post. *From 1906 to 1910 he worked at the* Rocky Mountain News. *During this period he met his future wife Ellen Egan, did chalk talks and stunt tours with Doc Bird Finch, and visited Pueblo, his home. By 1910 he had moved to New York City and returned home no more.*

Known first for his sports columns, and then for his "The Brighter Side" articles and short stories, Runyon was famous for his Broadway local color characters. New Yorkers forgot his Pueblo roots, and that Sky Madison of Guys *and* Dolls *was patterned after Bat Masterson, whom Runyon first knew of in connection with the Royal Gorge war and the roundhouse battle in Pueblo. In later years New York City may have been his home, but his roots were in Pueblo, Colorado. Photograph courtesy of the Pueblo Library District*

James Bradley Orman, 1901

Pueblo's mayor for 1897-98 had already been elected to the Colorado General Assembly in 1880, and the Colorado Senate from 1881 to 1885. The mayor was James Bradley Orman. Born November 4, 1849, at Muscatine, Iowa, Orman came to Colorado by mule train, arriving in 1868. Living first in Denver and then in Pueblo, Orman was one of the most prominent railroad contractors in the West.

Beginning with the contract of the Kansas Pacific Railroad between Sheridan and Denver, Orman was involved in the building of nearly all the important railroads in the state. The Colorado Midland between Colorado Springs and Aspen, the Florence and Cripple Creek road, and a considerable portion of the Colorado Springs and Cripple Creek road for the Denver and Rio Grande were his construction projects.

Orman participated in diversification before it was known as a business practice. During his career he was president of the Bessemer Ditch Company, a member of the Pueblo Opera House Company, and held mining interests in the Leadville, Ouray, Ashcroft, and Cottonwood districts. Photograph courtesy of the Pueblo Library District

Alva Adams

Alva Adams, 1850-1922, had many interests. He was a partner in Holmes Hardware Company, organizer of the Pueblo Savings and Trust Company, a director of the Standard Fire Brick Company, and one of the principal forces behind the growth of Pueblo as a community. A Democrat, he was elected governor of Colorado three times, serving in that office from 1887 to 1889, from 1897 to 1899, and for sixty-six days in 1905. Although he had been elected by a substantial majority, the election was questioned, and the legislature declared that Adams had been defeated. Adams served as governor until March 16, 1905. He died on November 1, 1922, and is buried in Roselawn Cemetery. Photograph courtesy of the Pueblo Library District

Orman Black on Union Avenue, 1888

In 1901 James Orman was elected governor of the state of Colorado. His election was credited to his role as the largest employer of laborers in the state due to his many enterprises. Orman died

July 21, 1919. Today the home that he built in 1890 at 102 West Orman Avenue is included on the National Register of Historic Places. It was also the home of Governor Alva Adams's family and used by School District 60 as a school administration building. Photograph courtesy of the Pueblo Library District

Pueblo Flood of 1894, Central Block in the Background

There have been floods in Pueblo in 1844, 1864, 1867, 1869, 1875, 1880, 1881, 1889, 1893, 1894, 1921, 1935, and 1965. On July 26, 1893, heavy rain broke the levee, and $200,000 in damages resulted. Water rushed through the break, and in ten minutes city hall was surrounded by six feet of water. Many of the early records of the city were lost, including the complete record of deaths which had been begun in 1892 by the city physician, Dr. Will B. Davis.

Following the flood of 1894 the levee system along the Arkansas River received major improvements. Photograph courtesy of the Pueblo Library District

Flood of 1894

The following account of the May 30, 1894, flood was printed in the Rocky Mountain News:

> *In consequence of all-day downpour of rain such as has not occurred in this valley in 20 years, the Arkansas River came up and broke the levees in four places on the north side and two on the south side. Everything is a sea of water from Union Avenue viaduct to the post office. All business cellars are filled in that territory, and the water is over the floors from 6 inches to 2 feet. This is a worse flood than any that has occurred since the town became a city. The water flows with a strong current through the streets, and everything is confusion. The flood covers the city from Union Avenue on the south side to Fourth Avenue on the north side, an area of three-quarters of a mile.*

Five lives were lost, and nearly $2 million damage was done to property. Photograph courtesy of the Pueblo Library District

The Atchison, Topeka and Santa Fe Railroad Depot After the Flood of 1894

Pueblo has survived a series of floods over the years. Early settlers recalled a flood in 1844 which, according to their testimony, was greater than the flood of 1921. Regular observations of the water stages of the Arkansas River began in 1885 at Rock Canyon, nine miles above Pueblo. After the 1894 flood, pictured here, the Colorado state engineer established a gauging station in Pueblo. Photograph courtesy of the Pueblo Library District

Fitts Manufacturing Company, Circa 1900

The 1899 city election was the first in which women ran for Pueblo elected offices. Mrs. Nellie W. Heller ran for city auditor on the Republican ticket. Fay R. Rockwell, Republican, and Mary Shimner, Socialist, ran for alderman. None of the women were elected. Angenette Peavey had been elected superintendent of public instruction for Colorado in 1895, so their hopes were not unrealistic.

The Fitts Manufacturing Company, known for its baking powder, was an important employer of women. Photograph courtesy of the Pueblo Library District

St. Anthony's Catholic Church, 1912

In 1899, Reverend Adalbert Blatnik, a native of Slovakia, came to assist in the ministry of St. Mary's Catholic Church. He concentrated his ministry on the Slovenians. In 1911 a new church was formed and ground purchased on Clark and C streets to build St. Anthony's Catholic Church. Building began in August 1911. Photograph courtesy of the Pueblo Library District

Pueblo Women in the Labor Force

1870—PUEBLO, COLORADO
Population: 2,265.

One woman in every 283 residents was employed. One out of every eleven residents was an immigrant.

Largest cultural group: New Mexicans.

Occupations for women: dometic servants, housekeepers.

1880
Population: 7,617.

One woman in every sixty residents was employed. One out of every nine residents was an immigrant.

Largest immigrant groups: German Empire, Irish, English-Welsh.

Occupations for women: domestic servants, dressmakers, boardinghouse proprietors, washerwomen.

1890
Population: 31,491.

Population growth for the city: 663.4 percent.

For every woman there were 1.76 men. One out of every five residents was an immigrant.

Largest immigrant groups: (in 1885) Irish, German, English.

Occupations for women: dressmakers, domestics, boardinghouse proprietors, laundresses, waitresses, clerks, teachers (nineteen).

1900
Population: 34,448.

For every woman there were 1.23 men.

55.3 percent of the population of the city were immigrants or first-generation Americans.

Largest immigrant groups: Austrian, Italian, German.

Occupations for women: teachers, domestics, clerks, dressmakers, waitresses, stenographers, renters of furnished rooms.

The First Colorado Coal and Iron Company Hospital, Circa 1881

*T*he history of Minnequa/Corwin Hospital can be traced to 1881, when the Colorado Coal and Iron Company engaged Dr. R. W. Corwin to come to Colorado to set up a medical department. The first hospital was built on the grounds of the Minnequa plant of the company. The original company hospital contained only six rooms for both hospital and dispensary use. The nursing force consisted of Dr. Corwin and two practical male nurses who came from Chicago with Dr. Corwin.

In 1882 a sickness near epidemic proportions developed among the steelworkers; a mild form of typhoid fever ran to 133 cases alone, and the little hospital was too small to care for them. That fall the Colorado Coal and Iron Company and the Denver and Rio Grande Railroad together built a hospital to accommodate thirty patients. This was the structure that later became the Casa Verde Apartments. In 1890 capacity was increased to forty-five beds. In 1895 an operating room and dispensary were added at a cost of $4,000. In 1897 a new wing was built, increasing bed capacity to eighty. Photograph courtesy of the Pueblo Library District

**Minnequa Hospital Nurses'
Graduating Class of 1905**

The first pupils came to the nurses' training school in 1899 for a three-year training program.

The year 1901 saw the selection of an approximately forty-acre site near Lake Minnequa for the erection of a new hospital. All buildings were of Spanish style. The number of cases hospitalized that year was 751.

The new 200-bed Minnequa Hospital was opened to the public August 2, 1902, and was occupied the following day by patients.

In 1903 nurses' hours were from 7 a.m. to 7 p.m., with intermissions for two meals and two hours for rest and recreation in the open air.

Dr. R. W. Corwin died June 19, 1929, and at the time of his death the name of the hospital was changed in his honor. Dr. William Senger became chief surgeon.

On February 17, 1948, the board of C.F.&I. voted overwhelmingly in favor of giving the hospital to the Sisters of Charity of Cincinnati, Ohio. A token payment of one dollar was made, and Corwin Hospital became St. Mary Corwin Hospital. Photograph courtesy of the Pueblo Library District

Minnequa Hospital, Circa 1902

There were no elevators or stairways in the entire hospital. All floors had an exit via a steel ramp to the outside in case of disaster. There were no private rooms, only two-bed and four-bed wards. Bath facilities were limited to one bathroom for men and one for women on each floor with only toilet and washbowl facilities. There were no bathtubs in the hospital. Photograph courtesy of the Pueblo Library District

**Minnequa Dispensary at the
Steelworks, Circa 1902**

*The Colorado Coal and Iron Company
assessed each of its employees a monthly
fee of one dollar to pay its share of the
hospital's operating expense and to main-
tain dispensaries in the mining camps.*

*The Minnequa dispensary at the steel-
works served to prevent sickness and to
administer promptly to ailments which, if
neglected, might prove serious. Physicians
and attendants were on duty twenty-four
hours a day.*

*In 1902 the dispensary handled 23,000
cases. Photograph courtesy of the Pueblo
Library District*

Chapter Five
Ethnicity

Two boys Selling Newspaper and Magazines

Over 127 newspapers have been published in Pueblo; of these, thirty have been foreign-language newspapers. The Freie Press, *a German-language newspaper, was the earliest known. The* Vox Populi, *thought to have been in Italian, was actually written in English.*

The United States Census has a column for literacy. It is concerned only with literacy in the English language. Pueblo's foreign language newspapers are proof of a literate immigrant population. Photograph courtesy of Gladys Hassey

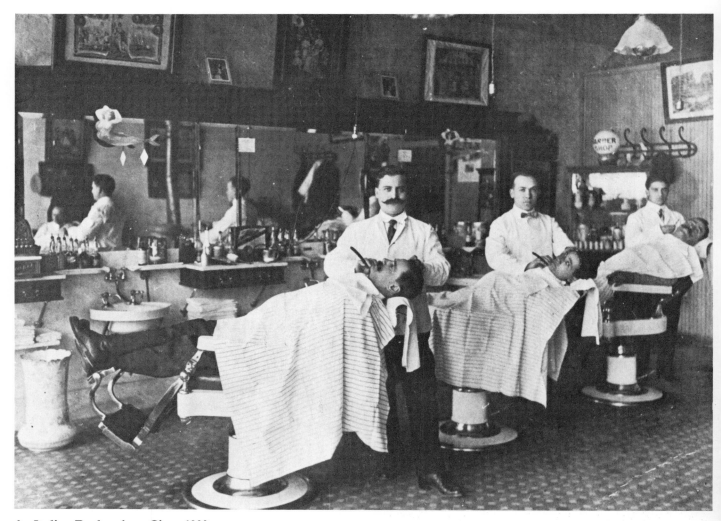

An Italian Barbershop, Circa 1900

*P*ueblo's immigration pattern followed that of the rest of the United States. Northern Europeans dominated in the 1870s and 1880s because those countries were experiencing large emigrations. When Pueblo was experiencing its greatest growth in the 1890s southern Europeans were emigrating. Photograph courtesy of Russell Battaglia

All of the citizens of the United States share one common bond—everyone immigrated to this land from somewhere else. It was not until 1819 that any effort was made by the government to record the arrival of immigrants. People simply disembarked from their ship onto the streets of the United States. Each new group enriched America, and although the details of their stories vary, all shared the bond of being strangers in a new land.

Farming by Steel Plow in Pueblo County

The introduction of the steel plow meant that one man could till what it had taken two men to do with a wooden plow. Unemployment was a major factor in the decision to come to America. Nevertheless, the average Pueblo immigrant did not come to stay. Many made two or three trips to their homeland before they decided to stay in the United States. Often the wife and children remained in the home village for years while the husband commuted back and forth. Photograph courtesy of Gladys Hassey

Denver and Rio Grande Railraod, Eighth Street Station, Circa 1900

The railroads sold land to immigrants at the points of entry, such as Ellis Island, and to workmen on the railroad. Frequently, new arrivals had little idea of the geography of America. Letters from Europe asked if Pueblo was near Chicago. Their concept of geography was changed by the length of time they spent on the train before arriving at the Denver and Rio Grande Eighth Street Station in Pueblo. Photograph courtesy of the Pueblo Library District

A Pueblo County Farm, Circa 1900

Cooperative, extended family homesteads were common. Immigrants from the same country homesteaded in one area. On arriving in the United States they would first work either for one of the smelters or for the Colorado Fuel and Iron Company. When a nest egg had been gathered the family would homestead. Once homesteading requirements had been completed, many of the families sold the farms and returned to better jobs in the cities. Several Swedish families lived in the Mustang area, other English immigrants settled near the Livesey brothers ranch, and Juanita was a Hispanic community. Photograph courtesy of the Pueblo Library District

Max Stein and His Partner Selling Pineapples

The earliest record of the Jewish community in Pueblo appeared in the American Israelite *on August 10, 1877. In a letter from M.M.E. the meeting to form a women's society was recorded. About twelve Jewish families were residing in Pueblo. The members of the new society were Mrs. Isaac Freund, Mrs. S. Rich, Mrs. M. Studginsky, Mrs. M. Bergman, Mrs. I. Gorden, Mrs. M. Nusbaum, Mrs. J. Louise, Mrs. R. Nusbaum, Mrs. S. Nathan, Mrs. F. Arkust, and Mrs. A. Goldsmith. In March 1882 the Independent Order of B'nai B'rith was formed under the name of the Twin City Lodge No. 331 of the Second Division.*

By 1883 the Jewish community was actively contributing to the Russian refugees at Cotopaxi. (Many of Pueblo's early Jewish citizens were from Russia.) In May 1885 the Hebrew Benevolent Union was formed to help the needy. On September 7, 1900, Rabbi E. G. Hirsh of Chicago delivered the dedicatory sermon for Temple Emanuel, according to the American Israelite. *Max Stein, a prominent businessman and member of the Jewish community, is on the right. Photograph courtesy of John Suhay*

Immigrant Freighters

The introduction of a simple factor can significantly change history. The arrival of railroads in southern Europe in the late 1800s displaced the freighters. If a person had lived in one region all his life, whether he moved 500 or 5,000 miles made little difference. The Beulah marble quarry freight system, which took three days for a round trip to Pueblo, provided jobs for displaced European freighters. Photograph courtesy of C. W. Donley

Farmers Delivering Sugar Beets to the Railroad, Circa 1895

The sugar beet industry in the eastern portion of the county employed Germans from Russia. In 1762 and 1763, Catherine the Great of Russia had issued two special manifestos inviting foreigners to settle in Russia. Religious freedom, free transportation to Russia, perpetual exemption from military and civil service, interest-free loans to buy land, and eighty free acres of land were offered. German peasants from Hesse and the Rhineland, recovering from crop failures and the Seven Years' War, responded and settled along the Volga River in central Russia. In 1871 Alexander II, the great-grandson of Catherine the Great, revoked many of the German colonists' inherited privileges. The czar sought to assimilate the German colonies and required that Russian be taught in the schools. Emigration from the German colonies in Russia began. By the 1880s Germans from Russia were settling in Colorado in large numbers. The sugar beet industry provided employment. Mothers and fathers, daughters and sons all worked together in the fields. Photograph courtesy of the Pueblo Library District

A. Quaranta's Italian Royal Band, Circa 1910

The emigration of Italians to the United States is related to two major events in Italian history. The revolution of 1848 precipitated the exodus of the intellectuals and the anti-clericals, primarily from northern Italy. In the 1880s opposition to the new unified Italy and the subsequent loss of local government control stimulated the migration of southern Italians. Photograph courtesy of the Pueblo Library District

An Italian Family Living on Smelter Hill, 1903

On *February 26, 1885, the United States Congress prohibited the importation and migration of foreigners and aliens under contract or agreement to perform labor in the United States. Prior to 1885 American industry had sent representatives to Europe to hire cheap labor. The new law did not stop industry from advertising in Europe. Immigrants caught at ports of entry with a contract for a job were sent home. New Orleans, Louisiana, and Galveston, Texas, were popular ports of entry for immigrants headed for Pueblo. An Italian family living on Smelter Hill is shown. Photograph courtesy of the Pueblo Library District*

Early View of Smelter Hill

The area originally identified as a Mexican settlement in 1888 was becoming a squatters' community by the 1890s. Known as Smelter Hill or Old Mexico these temporary homes provided shelter for various ethnic groups who worked in the smelters or the steelworks. Photograph courtesy of the Pueblo Library District

Smelter Hill A Few Years Later

Smelter Hill, Pepper Sauce Bottoms, and Salt Creek were all squatters' communities. Squatters were people who settled without any right or title on another person's land. In Pueblo most of the squatters lived on public land or on property owned by their employers. The random layout of the housing demonstrates the unplanned growth of the communities. Photograph courtesy of the Pueblo Library District

A Later View of Smelter Hill

Many immigrants had just enough money to travel to the United States. These temporary homes were one of the steps to a better life. Each new wave of immigrants pushed the previous group of immigrants up the socioeconomic ladder. One example in Pueblo was the Irish, who became the bosses on the railroads and supervised later immigrants. Photograph courtesy of the Colorado Historical Society

According to oral interviews, this is what the interior of a squatter's home might have looked like. Photograph courtesy of Gladys Hassey

St. Mary Church, Original

In 1891 Bishop Nicholas Matz of Denver asked Reverend Boniface Wimmer, founder of the Benedictine order in this country, to establish a parish for all the German-speaking people of the city. St. Mary began when an abandoned broom factory was purchased and converted into a church building.

In 1894 the new pastor took a census. He counted about 800 Slovenes and nearly 500 Slovaks. Children were mighty few,

ladies very rare, but young men from twenty to thirty proportionally a great many.

In 1895 ground was purchased on Clark Street to build a more spacious church building. In a few months the church was erected. A school run by the Benedictine Sisters was on the first floor and the church was on the second.

After heavy damage during the 1921 flood, the church purchased from the

Newton Lumber Company half of the defunct Eiler Smelter Works off South Santa Fe and East Mesa avenues.

Remodeling and construction of the new church and school buildings began. St. Mary was the parent church for St. Boniface, St. Leander, and St. Anthony churches. Photograph courtesy of the Pueblo Library District

The interior of St. Mary Church, Christmas 1896. Photograph courtesy of the Pueblo Library District

The Protective and Benevolent Society of Pueblo, an Italian Lodge, 1930

The immigrant population usually was isolated from the general community. Many came as single men. Lodges and churches filled social and communication needs. In the era before social security the lodge's insurance plan, paid weekly, insured a decent funeral and emotional support for one's family. The story of the lady in a blue suit is a good example of the difficulties faced by immigrants.

I will always remember the time Luigi sent for a wife from the mail order house. One day he brought me the catalog, and showed me a picture of a handsome blue-eyed blond, dressed in a navy blue suit. It was some time before I understood what was wanted, but at length I understood. Luigi wanted me to write a letter to the mail order house, ordering the girl in the picture. In vain I explained to him that it was the suit that was $24.97 and not the girl. He insisted until I wrote the letter for him. He evidently enclosed the money in cash and mailed the letter immediately. The next day he was at the post office looking for his bride, and for every day thereafter, until at last a package arrived for him. But, alas, it was only the suit. Luigi came to me greatly excited, and again showed me the picture.

'I want the wife first, then the dress. You tell this book they make a mistake.' I could not make him understand, but finally had him return the suit for a refund of his money. Every time Luigi sees me, he sighs and shakes his head. I know he thinks that I didn't write the letter as it should have been, otherwise, he would have had his bride.

(Works Progress Administration of Colorado oral interviews project, 1934).

Father Cyril Zupan, Circa 1890s

Reverend Cyril Zupan (seated on the right) was the second pastor at St. Mary Church. A native of Carniola, he served from 1894 to 1939. He not only understood and spoke the same language as his congregation, he understood their heritage. The peasants had not been liberated in Austria until 1848. Land which previously had been owned by landlords was then available for purchase. It took twenty to twenty-five years to pay for the land. It was not until the mid-1870s that they were free to migrate. Photograph courtesy of the Pueblo Library District

A Japanese "Picture Bride," Before and After, Circa 1900

The Japanese mail-order bride was known as a picture bride. Her experiences were the same as her European counterpart. The primary difference would have been that the Japanese bride's parents would have arranged the marriage instead of the young lady. Both photographs are of the same woman, Hanaye Todoo Kameoka. The second photograph shows her with her husband Frank Kumaichiro Kameoka and daughter Myrtle Hinako. Photograph courtesy of the Pueblo Library District

Italian Woman Baking Bread, 1905

The following 1936 WPA interview with an Italian mail-order bride is representative of many immigrant women's stories. Frequently the bride-to-be would spend a few days with mutual friends or work at a boardinghouse until the marriage.

I had twenty-eight years and prayed every day to the Virgin to give me a husband, but all the young man from my village had come to America, so I ask the priest if he could find a good man in America for me. Then he showed me when the month had turned, a letter from Giano in America, who came from Venetia, and asked for a wife. Giano sent also his picture, and I told the priest, 'It is good! I will start to America when you arrange it.'

On the boat were many girls coming to America to marry, but none so far as Colorado. But I had no fear as the Santissima Mary would not let me suffer. I brought with me a wedding ring, as I did not know where Indians lived if they would have the proper bands for the marriage. When I come to the house which Giano has fixed there is a stove, but no pans. I ask Giano, 'How can I fix the polenta and stew without the pans?' Giano say, 'I get them.' There was a bed with good springs, and I tell Giano, 'It is good!'

We were married . . . and afterward had a—what you call it—celebration for two days. Then I had to wash, as the clothes were dirty, but there were no tubs. I tell Giano and he say, 'I get them.' So I work, work, and have babies—one every year. But, Santissima, it is what I pray for in Italy.

Photograph courtesy of the Pueblo Library District

By 1890 Pueblo had 31,491 residents, with a growth rate of 663.4% for the decade. One out of every five Puebloans was an immigrant. A. F. DeVry, the agent for the German and Austrian consulates resided at 223 East Fifth Street.

Americanization was an important aspect of country school education. Photograph courtesy of Pueblo Library District

Room One at Riverside School, Located Near City Hall, Circa 1900

Immigrant children who could not speak English were kept in the first and second grades until they could. Most of the children learned very quickly. At some of the country schools, the teacher would allow immigrant children to come to school a year early so they could learn the language and start with the other children who were their age. Many immigrant children attended Riverside School. Photograph courtesy of the Pueblo Library District

A Unit of the Austrian Conscription Army, 1901

By 1900, 55.3 percent of the residents of the city were immigrants or first-generation Americans. The 1,282 Austrians were the largest group, followed by 761 Italians, 746 Germans, 518 Irish, 478 Swedish, 466 English, and 432 Canadians. The Austrians included people from all parts of the Austrian empire—Slovenia, Croatia, and other countries now included in Yugoslavia.

Involuntary enlistment in the Austrian military was a fact of life in the Austrian empire. Many young men opted to come to the United States instead.

Jan Mendork, a Pole, served in this unit of the Austrian conscription army in 1901. Photograph courtesy of the Pueblo Library District

Hispanic Residents of Pueblo County in the 1900s

The Hispanic population, which had decreased during the 1880s and 1890s, began to increase at the turn of the century. Pueblo's earliest Hispanic residents had been from New Mexico and *were among the first settlers. The new Hispanic settlers were primarily from Mexico. Photograph courtesy of the Pueblo Library District*

An Austrian Workbook, 1905

A workbook was another aspect of life in the Austrian empire. All adults had workbooks which listed the jobs they had held and references. This is the workbook of Johanna Chujeba, who came to America to escape workbooks just as others came to avoid the conscription army. Immigrants who came to Pueblo, regardless of their nationality, came to Pueblo to improve their life. Photograph courtesy of the Pueblo Library District

John Poulos, a Greek Resident of Pueblo, 1916

John Rougas departed for the United States from Greece with four cousins on February 28, 1907. They each paid eighty dollars to go from Patras, Greece, to Kansas City, Kansas. They sailed on the Celtic, which belonged to the White Star Line. It took eleven days to go from Naples to New York City. They stayed overnight at Ellis Island, and the next day they passed the physical examination. The following day they bought a package of food including bread, bananas, and beef salami or bologna for one dollar. They then boarded another ship, which took them to Baltimore, Maryland. Next they took the train to Kansas City. The cousin who was supposed to be in Kansas City had moved to Linn, New Mexico. Rougas came to Pueblo because it had a Greek church.

A friend of Rougas, John Poulos, is shown on March 25, 1916, Greek Independence Day, in the Greek honor guard uniform. Photograph courtesy of the Pueblo Library District

Hellenic Orthodox Church of St. John the Baptist

This church is located on the corner of Spruce Street and Summit Avenue and is one of the oldest Greek Orthodox churches in the United States. Photograph by Edwin L. Dodds

The Davenport, a Pueblo Boardinghouse, Circa 1920

The Davenport, 2137 East Evans Avenue, was leased by representatives of the Colorado Coal and Iron Company to individuals. Ida Hellund Charlson, the second person from the left in front of the porch, *was a Swedish widow with ten daughters who ran the boardinghouse from about 1919 to 1927. Before Mrs. Charlson ran it, the Davenport was a Japanese boardinghouse. The majority of Pueblo's Japanese population had returned to Japan at the instruction of the emperor due to the threat of war.*

To the right of Mrs. Charlson are seven of her daughters: and a friend named Tasha. Next are two boarders, Louis Larson and Pete Hanson. On the porch are Sig Carlson, A. B. Jones, Dahliv, an unidentified boy and man, and Olson. Photograph courtesy of the Pueblo Library District

Columbus Day Banquet, Columbus Hall on Northern Avenue, 1930

The Columbus Day banquet on October 12, 1930, celebrated the successful cooperation of Italians in Pueblo. L'Unione, the Italian-language weekly newspaper, published at 320-322 South Victoria Avenue, *is credited with being the best Italian-language newspaper published in the United States. Based upon the foundations laid by Hector Chiariglione and his partner Joseph Battaglia, Vincent Massari led the newspaper to national prominence. Photograph courtesy of the Pueblo Library District*

**Cedarwood, Colorado,
Which Received Postal Service
From 1912 to 1943**

The existence of a post office indicates more than mere mail delivery. Every post office in Pueblo County records the exis- tence of a community. Some of the com- munities exist today; however, most have disappeared. The missing communities are the ghost towns of Pueblo County. The Cedarwood schoolhouse can be seen at the center of the photograph. Photo- graph by Edwin L. Dodds

Pueblo County Post Offices

Abbey	same place as Muddy Creek, 1891-1914
Agate	1880-81
Airport	established as a rural station of Pueblo, 1953-55
Andersonville	1868-69
Arland	1895
Armour	1886-92
Artman	1892-1901
Avondale	1892
Beaver	formerly named Beaver Creek, originally named Toof
Beaver Creek	?
Beulah	formerly Mace's Hole, 1876
Boone	1891
Booneville	1863-91
Bronquist	1917-25
Burnt Mill	formerly Kinkel, 1911-21
Cedarwood	1912-43
Chilcott	1884-90
Colorado City	1964
Cousin Springs	(Cozzens) 1914-20
Crow	1885-91, 1896-1907
Dawkins	post office moved to Pinon, 1885-1907
Duke	1908
Eden	1890-1914
Excelsior	1866, 1867-71
Fisher	1895-1908
Foothills	1921-27
Fort Reynolds	1869-70
Goodpasture	1895-1923
Graneros	1889-1925
Greenhorn	1897-1911
Grimaldi	1913-1920
Haynes Ranch	1861-63
Hermosilla	1870-72
Holden	1892-93
Huerfano	post office moved from Apache, 1882-83, 1883-84, 1900-29
Juniata	1869-93
Keble	1899
Kinkle	name changed to Burnt Mill, 1907-11

Lamar	1885-86
Lebanon	1875-76
Lees	1897-1904
Lime	1898-1943
Mace's Hole	name changed to Beulah, 1873-76
Marnel	1917-23
Mercier	1906-13
Muddy Creek	1870-86
Myrtle	1906-13
Nepesta	1876-1929
North Avondale	1917
Nyburg	1889-1918
Osage	1884-88, earlier as Osage Avenue
Osage Avenue	1873-82
Overton	1892-1900
Pinon	1907-21
Pueblo West	1969
Rock Creek	1909-15
Rye	1881
Saint Charles	1866-76
Salt Creek	1880-93
Siloam	1891-1943
Sitton	1906-17
South Pueblo	1874-87
South Side	1869-77
Sparrow	1883-85
Sperryvale	1901
Stone City	1912-57, formerly named Cabin Springs
Swallows	post office moved from Taylorville, 1892-96, 1926-47
Table Mountain	1879-80
Tacony	1915-42
Taylorville	post office moved to Swallows, 1878-92
Undercliffe	1879-1925, formerly Huerfano
Verde	1903-12
Waremont	1916-22
White Rock	1909-27
Wilson	1911-13
Wood Valley	1862-65

The list was abstracted from William H. Bauer's Colorado Postal History.

The settlement of the county occurred in five stages. The first two settlement patterns were directly related to the rivers and streams which provided needed moisture. The pioneer settlements of Charles Autobees, Charles Doyle, and others primarily from northern New Mexico were first. The gold rush agricultural boom was next. Early homesteaders were able to grow two crops per season by relying on rainfall and the water table to provide moisture.

The arrival of the railroads created the third settlement phase. At set intervals communities were created and the land sold to prospective farmers. The sale by the railroads of land adjacent to their tracks explained why one portion of the county would be settled and not another.

The development of the railroad communities increased the need for irrigation. By 1883, 92,422 acres were under irrigation, which was more irrigated acreage than in any other Colorado county. As the number of canals increased new farming communities developed, and the fourth settlement phase emerged. One of the clearest indications of this pattern was in the area that the first communities (such as Autobees) were located. Since the railroads were built on the north side of the river, development on the south side had suffered. It was not until the development of the irrigation systems that this area became more densely populated.

The fifth factor in the settlement of the county was caused by a series of changes in the homesteading laws which allowed people to claim larger tracts of land. The railroads offered special services called immigrant trains. A freight car loaded with a settler's personal and agricultural goods could be sidetracked at an appointed destination. Next, freighters would haul a settler's goods to the homestead. The regulations for homesteading were written for moist regions. Colorado farmers were forced to break the soil, thus contributing to the dust bowl of the 1930s and the decreased settlement of the county.

A Farm in the Community Known as Foothills, Located near Doyle, Colorado

The 1930 census recorded Colorado's population as 1,035,791 with 27.3 percent living on 59,956 farms. Most of them had been homesteaded. The Homestead Act, signed by President Lincoln on May 27, 1862, authorized any citizen or intended citizen to select any surveyed but unclaimed tract of public land up to 160 acres and to gain title of it after five years of residence, making prescribed improvements, and paying a modest fee for the service of the registrar and receiver. If the homesteader wanted to gain title at the end of six months, he could commute his homestead entry to a preemption entry, pay $1.25 an acre, and receive title to it. In 1916 full-section homesteads were permitted on land suitable for grazing. People farmed in regions that should not have been farmed. The rate of failure was high. The community known as Foothills is one that failed. Photograph courtesy of the Pueblo Library District

Beulah Blacksmith Shop on Grand Avenue

The Beulah blacksmith shop was a busy and popular place. Stories of Beulah's past were told to summer residents and retold to valley residents. The first land patent granted in the area was to Anna M. Sease on June 10, 1872. Earlier the area was the hideout of Juan Mace a dashing Hispanic cattle thief. To discourage pursuit, Mace left anonymous letters on the plains, where herders would be sure to find them, indicating that he had a large band. The area where he hid the stolen cattle became known as Mace's Hole.

During the Civil War, Mace's Hole was the secret recruit camp for Confederates. Outside the valley, near Turtle Buttes, was buried the Solid Muldoon hoax, purported to be the petrified body of a prehistoric species resembling both

man and ape. The perpetrator of the hoax was George Hull, with P. T. Barnum as a partner. The Solid Muldoon was discovered September 16, 1877. Before the hoax was exposed the Muldoon, named after a popular song of the period, was exhibited from Council Bluffs, Iowa, to New York City. Photograph courtesy of C. W. Donley

Balanced Rock

To escape the heat of summer, many prominent Puebloans had summer homes in Beulah. The Balanced Rock was one of the sights for summer visitors. Photograph courtesy of Pueblo Library District

Beulah Marble Quarry, Circa 1900

Beulah Red marble, located in the west end of the valley, was used as the wainscoting for the Colorado State Capitol. The work of quarrying the stone was done by driving steel wedges into a series of hand-drilled holes, causing the marble to break off without extensive danger or loss. Machinery was hand operated and heavy wooden derricks and winches were used to move and load the blocks. A similar quarrying method was used at Stone City. Photograph courtesy of the Pueblo Library District

Beulah School, 1887

The first Beulah public school was located at the northeast corner of the intersection of Fox Lane and Pine Drive. Notice that children from the same family are wearing the same fabric. Mother made the clothes, and frequently she purchased one bolt of material for the entire family.

This 1887 photograph includes, in the front row, from left to right seated: Anna and Maude Goodpasture, Lizzie and Jennie Curtis, Edna Lizzie, and Susie Sease, Anna Burns, Ella Boggs, Maybelle Lewis, Anna and Nettie Sease, Esther and Lenore Sellers, Robert Marshall (standing) and an unidentified boy visitor. Second row: Oliver Evarts, Sam Curtis, Frank Curtis, Adam Goodpasture, Malita Sease, Frankie Patton, Jeanette Evarts, Gale Tony, Christian Burns, John Burns, Joe Patton, Henry Berry, and Virgil Boggs. Back row: Lee Hughlett, Dave Lewis, George and Egbert Sease, Calvin Boggs, Alvin Lewis, Bert Evarts, Edson Sellers, and the teacher, Mr. Lunnon. Photograph courtesy of C. W. Donley

Carl Goss, From the Butler Ranch, Demonstrating a Popular Method of School Transportation Before Consolidation

The location of the school was an important community issue. One schoolhouse in the Pinon area was moved so frequently that the building was left on skids. In District 70, before consolidation, one family solved the problem of an inconvenient school location by transferring. The reason given was that the boy had to get off his horse three times to open and close gates on the way to school. The adjoining district's school would only require the boy to dismount to open and close one gate. The petition was granted. Photograph courtesy of the Pueblo Library District

Goodpasture, Colorado, 1895-1923

Lee Roper is viewed as the founder of Goodpasture, Colorado. He arrived in the area in the late 1880s. As others settled, the Roper family began enterprises to serve the area. The community included Cedar Grove school, Goodpasture Methodist Church, a general store, a post office from 1895 to 1923, and later a blacksmith shop. The advertisement touts the Rood Candy Company of Pueblo. The community was named for William Goodpasture, a Beulah resident, who had helped Roper set up the post office. Photograph courtesy of the Pueblo Library District

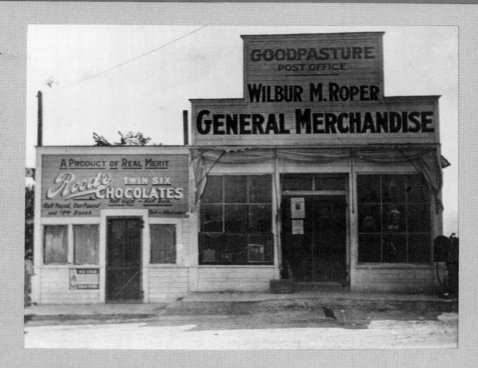

Farabaugh Family on the Way to Pueblo From Turkey Creek, Circa 1910

Georgia Farabaugh, the first Pueblo woman to be appointed mayor, lived between 1898 and 1917 in the Turkey Creek area.

The Farabaugh family is shown on one of their trips to Pueblo for supplies. Her parents had homesteaded 160 acres just above the future site of Teller Reservoir. The railroad went only as far as Stone City, and the post office was at Myrtle.

Four hired men and four miners lived with the ten-member family. They hauled fire clay (used by Colorado Fuel and Iron Company to line ovens) down to the railroad at Swallows, until the Colorado-Kansas Railroad was built. While the reservoir was being built they hauled grain.

When it was time to attend high school the children moved to town and lived with their grandmother. Generally rural schools taught grades one through eight. Many rural children boarded in Pueblo in order to attend high school. Photograph courtesy of the Pueblo Library District

The Cheesemaker, Mr. McCasky, Circa 1916

*T*he entire output of the Cedar Grove Cheese Factory was sold to the Colorado Supply Company. Photograph courtesy of Alice Hull

Cedar Grove Cheese Factory, Circa 1916

*F*rom 1914 to 1917 the Cedar Grove Cheese Factory served area dairymen and farmers having surplus milk. Living quarters were on the second floor. Photograph courtesy of Ruth Eden Roper

Crow, Colorado, Now a Part of Colorado City

*C*row, Colorado, named for a family with the surname Crow, served as a rest stop on the way to Pueblo from Table Mountain/Rye. The average trip to Pueblo took four days. It took one day to come down the hill, another day to travel to Pueblo, and two days to make the return trip. Photograph courtesy of the Pueblo Library District

Rye, Colorado

Rye, originally known as Table Mountain, was renamed for the grain after postal authorities objected to the lengthy name. Photograph courtesy of the Pueblo Library District

An early view of downtown Rye, Circa 1900

Photograph courtesy of the Pueblo Library District

Swallows Railroad Depot, Circa 1920

Many Pueblo communities were railroad station communities. Frequently, they were named for whoever had owned the land before the railroad arrived, like Nyberg, or for a physical feature of the area such as Lime, Swallows, whose station appears here, Cedarwood, and Stone City. Photograph courtesy of the Pueblo Library District

Cape Horn Ranch, Circa 1890, Now a Part of Pueblo West

Charlie, the cook for the Cape Horn Ranch, was paid more than the cowboys because his day started earlier and ended later. The Cape Horn Ranch is now a part of Pueblo West. Photograph courtesy of the Pueblo Library District

Stockman's Hotel, Circa 1915

By 1915 barbed wire fences made cattle drives over what had been open range difficult. Instead, cattle were moved by train. The Stockmen's or Stockyard's Hotel on Joplin Street provided shelter for stockmen riding the cattle trains and for those who worked in the yards. Photograph courtesy of the Pueblo Library District

Children on Their Way Home From Vineland School, Circa 1910

Because the early railroad lines were located on the north side of the Arkansas River, the south side of the river developed more slowly. Vineland received its name from the local Italian farmers' grapevines. Many of the farms were begun by men who were working for the Colorado Fuel and Iron Company. During slow times, when there were layoffs, the men worked the farms.

The Vineland school district was one of the earliest Pueblo school districts to provide special classes for migrant children. Photograph courtesy of the Pueblo Library District

Letting Water Into a Side Sluice-Way, An Early Colorado Irrigation System

In 1909 Colorado ranked first among the states in irrigation with 2,790,000 acres so farmed. In 1918 agricultural production increased sharply to aid war needs. By 1920 the postwar depression hit the farms. Sugar beets were an important crop in southern Colorado. Photograph courtesy of the Pueblo Library District

Avondale, Colorado, Circa 1910

Sam Taylor, an Englishman, named Avondale, Colorado, for his old home, Stratford-on-Avon, England. Postal service began in 1892. Taylor started the Taylor Mercantile Company, shown here in 1894. Photograph courtesy of the Pueblo Library District

UIT OR OVERCOAT $15.

UNION MADE

EE WOOLEN MILLS

WHERE WE GET

OUR CLOTHS

FLOYD PHOTO.

A Dundee Woolen Mills Display

During the early years of the twentieth century, before the flood of 1921, Pueblo had more than fifty manufacturers who provided regular employment for more than 1,000 men throughout the year. This photo represents the many small manufacturers which existed in Pueblo prior to the flood of 1921. Photograph courtesy of John Suhay

Walter, Ford, Robert, and Dorothy Swearingen in 1917, Representing Family Life in Pueblo

The United States Census began keeping track of the number of dwellings in the city of Pueblo in 1880. The number of persons per dwelling decreased with each decade. In 1890 there were 3,410 dwellings with 6.53 persons to a family and 7.20 persons to a dwelling. By 1900 there were 6,928 dwellings and 4.5 persons to a family. In 1910 there were 8,655 dwellings and 4.8 persons to a family. In 1920 there were 8,956 dwellings and 4.1 persons to a family. Photograph courtesy of the Swearingen family

Dr. Louise Black

Genevieve Tucker, Anna Williams, Carrie Johnson, Josephine Nachtrieb, Mary F. Barry, Louise Black, Theresa L. Black, Ella Finch, and Josephine Myers were Pueblo physicians in 1900.

Louise Black, physician at the Clark Mineral Springs Hospital was an exceptionally tall woman. One evening on her way home from Union Avenue across the B Street Bridge to the Grove, she was accosted by a man. Dr. Black threw the man off the railroad bridge. There was no water to soften his fall. Dr. Black continued to walk in safety. Photograph courtesy of the Pueblo Library District

Doyle School, Circa 1890

Before the turn of the century many teachers were male. It was not until the 1900s that women began to dominate the field. Teaching was one of the few professions in which students could finance their own education. High school graduates were allowed to teach one year before receiving additional training. They taught during the school year and then spent their earnings to go to summer school. Photograph courtesy of the Pueblo Library District

Pueblo, with a diverse economic base, entered the new century as the second largest city in the state. While the smelting industry was declining, the steel works had undergone tremendous growth and improvement under the ownership of John C. Osgood. The industrial foundations laid by the railroads had flourished. The Nuckolls Packing Plant, the Dundee Woolen Mills, the Rood Candy Company, the Fitts Manufacturing Company, and a score of other small industries prospered.

A tremendous boom in real estate had occurred after consolidation. It would not be until the 1950s that the areas platted during the boom would be occupied. Isolated neighborhoods, such as Irving Place, were developed. Blende and Bessemer were growing, and the trolley car system was tying the community together. No longer did laborers and businessmen need to walk to work. This allowed greater freedom in the selection of housing. Main Street and Northern Avenue were replacing Santa Fe and Union avenues as the business districts. Clerks and businessmen from the downtown area lived in the newly developed Eastside, formerly the site of Fountain City. The foundations for a great city had been laid and Pueblo was ready.

McClelland Public Library, Circa 1910

In 1868 Pueblo's first library was established on Santa Fe Avenue. The Pueblo Library Association was formed in 1873, when public-spirited citizens purchased the 200 shares of stock at fifty dollars a share. The association did not survive, and the books were given to the county jail. On April 10, 1891, the McClelland Library opened on the fourth floor of the Board of Trade building. The library was named for Andrew McClelland because of his $6,000 gift to the library. The city of Pueblo added the library as a city function in 1893 and voted $3,000 annually for new books and librarians' salaries. In 1901 a committee appointed by the Monday Evening Club approached Andrew Carnegie with a request for a library building. On January 19, 1904, the McClelland Public Library opened with a collection of 1,072 books. The Royal Park site was convenient to all the citizens of Pueblo. Photograph courtesy of the Pueblo Library District

The Pueblo Colorado Supply Company Store, Circa 1900

Company scrip was accepted at the Colorado Supply Company retail store. Adjacent to the retail store was the warehouse for the entire network of stores which served the employees of the Colorado Fuel and Iron Company. Located on Canal Street, the buildings were built circa 1900. Photograph courtesy of the Pueblo Library District

The First McClelland Home for Children, 106 Lake Avenue

The McClelland Children's Home, known prior to 1927 as the McClelland Home for Children, began in 1905 when a group of concerned citizens organized as the Protestant Orphanage Committee. The first orphanage site for the organization was at 1104 East Routt Avenue, under the direction of four deaconesses of the Methodist Episcopal Church. The home opened with four children, but soon there were fifteen children. Larger quarters were needed.

Andrew McClelland offered the building that had been erected for a Southern Methodist Church College but never used, if $5,000 could be raised. A campaign was launched. When a lull in the fund raising occurred, Columbia Jane McClelland contributed the $5,000 from her own money. The board met and gave the orphanage the title of McClelland Home for Children. In 1932 plans were started for a new home. With substantial help from the Pueblo Rotary Club, the Georgian style building was occupied February 17, 1935. Photograph courtesy of the Pueblo Library District

Atchison, Topeka and Santa Fe Freight Depot

The depot, located on Union Avenue, could accommodate sixty-eight freight cars at one time. Built in 1902-03, it replaced the depot on Court Street. Photograph courtesy of the Pueblo Library District

137

Colorado State Hospital Superintendent's Residence and the Stewart's Cottage, Circa 1900

Dr. A. P. Busey stated in his 1904 annual report that asylums, to accomplish the most good and to be the most useful and beneficial to the insane, should be built on the cottage plan and arranged to accommodate not more than 500 patients at one institution. When more room is required a new institution should be established. He was opposed to restraint of any kind, and used it as little as consistent with the welfare of all.

On December 31, 1912, Dr. Busey resigned. On January 1, 1913, Dr. H. A. LaMoure, assistant superintendent, was promoted to the superintendency.

On September 27, 1899, Dr. Anna Williams of Denver was appointed physician in the women's department.

On April 10, 1917, the Colorado Insane Asylum at Pueblo became the Colorado State Hospital. Photograph courtesy of the Pueblo Library District

---

Some selected rules and regulations of the Colorado State Insane Asylum, December, 1889

1. The superintendent *"shall see that the patients are in the open air as much as possible."*
2. The druggist *"shall permit no loafing or card playing in the drug room."*
3. The two chief nurses *"shall rise, breakfast and be on duty at 6:30 a.m. . . .and remain on duty to 7:30 p.m."*
4. No person will be retained in the asylum service who is known to be a user of intoxicating liquors, who engages in gambling, or any immoral or disreputable practice.
5. No letter or writing of a patient shall be mailed or delivered without the consent of the superintendent.
6. The nurses *"shall give the patients ample time to eat and never send them from the table in less than 20 minutes."*
7. The two divisions of the institution (male and female) are always separate to its employees.
8. No one is permitted to enter the corridors, stairways, or basement rooms of the building of the opposite sex without the special order of a medical doctor.

Colorado State Hospital Dairy Herd, Circa 1900

Between the opening of the hospital in 1879 and 1900, 2,281 patients were admitted. Of these 973 were discharged recovered, 176 were discharged improved, 1 was discharged not insane, and 607 died.

In 1896 there were only eleven attendants in the asylum to take care of 422 patients.

Early therapy included participation in meaningful labor, such as farming and housekeeping. Photograph courtesy of the Pueblo Library District

The Brown Cabin After the 1901 Flood

In spring 1901 heavy rains caused flooding of the north section of Charles Creek near Beulah Hill. The John Brown family had moved to the valley earlier that year and settled in a two-story cabin a short distance west of Beulah Hill. Torrential rain caused the creek to rise very rapidly. The lower section of the cabin collapsed, and the top floor washed downstream until it lodged against some trees.

The following morning, two children were found huddled in the remains of the top section of the cabin shown here. An eyewitness recalled "The little girl told us her mother had a spell and Papa went down to get a rocker for her and he did not come back." The parents were buried in the Beulah Cemetery. Photograph courtesy of Mr. and Mrs. Darrell Clarke

Livestock on Parade at the Colorado State Fair, Circa 1910

In 1901 eighty new acres were purchased and the fair moved to its present location. The State Fair Association received its first state appropriation in 1903 to pay agricultural and horticultural premiums.

During the Depression the State Fair Association sponsored many Works Progress Administration projects utilizing native stone. Photograph courtesy of Gladys Hassey

Walter's Brewery on Joplin Street, Circa 1925

"Quench your thirst. Steady your nerves and cool your Brain with a glass of Pueblo Beer."

As early as 1902 Walter's Beer claimed to be Pueblo's beer. The brewing company had been in Pueblo since 1898, and this was their town. Not that competition was lacking. In 1904 Coors, Golden Beer, P. H. Zang, and Anheuser Busch companies all had agents in Pueblo. Over the years it was the Walter Brewing Company that became Pueblo's brewing company. At one time the firm was bottling beer for twenty-seven different brands distributed in seven western states. In 1974 the brewery closed. Photograph courtesy of the Pueblo Library District

139

**The Press Room of the *Star-Journal*,
219 East Grand Avenue**

*T*he first issue of the Star-Journal *was
published on June 1, 1901, after the
consolidation of two older newspapers,
the* Evening Star *and the* Pueblo Evening
Journal. *In 1904 the* Star-Journal *moved
to 219 East Grand Avenue. In 1933 the*
Chieftain *merged with the* Star-Journal.

*Both newspapers were published at the
Grand Avenue location until 1937. The*
Chieftain *and the* Star-Journal *moved to
their present location at 825 West Sixth
Street in 1961. Photograph courtesy of
Ralph Taylor*

**A *Star-Journal*-Sponsored
Baseball Team**

*Photograph courtesy of the Pueblo Library
District*

Lake Minnequa Amusement Park, Circa 1905

Adventure lay just within reach when one took the trolley to the Lake Minnequa Amusement Park. Opening each Memorial Day and closing in September, the park offered all the amusements one could desire. It all began on Friday, May 30, 1902, at 1:00 p.m. The newspaper described the opening thus: "Mid the booming of cannon and the playing of bands Lake Minnequa opened." Boating, bathing, fishing, boat races, fishing contests, a merry-go-round (now at Pueblo City Park), and booths that offered games of chance were available to the adventurer. By the following year a summer theater that seated 1,000 was added along with a roller coaster. Admission to the park was ten cents. Admission to the theater was extra, but all the other events went with the admission price. The trolley car company was so impressed with the park that they provided a trolley at the gate every five minutes. Photograph courtesy of Gladys Hassey

Honored Guests at the Annual Abraham Lincoln Dinner

In 1870 twenty-seven blacks lived in Pueblo County. By 1880 the number had increased to 141. Many black men were employed as barbers and cooks. The American Citizen, *published by James J. McClure, was the first black newspaper published in Pueblo, about 1903. M. B. Brooks was the managing editor of the* Colorado Times *in 1907, and it was published at 1312 East Evans Avenue. The* Rising Sun, *published by Thomas L. Cate, was the third black newspaper in Pueblo and was followed by M. O. Seymour's* Western Ideal. *The annual Abraham Lincoln dinner honored former slaves who lived in Pueblo County. Photograph courtesy of the Pueblo Library District*

Eden Train Wreck, 1904

On August 7, 1904, a cloudburst dumped huge amounts of water in the small basin drained by Hogan's Ditch. A torrent of water came rushing down the arroyo and washed out the wooden county road bridge. The wreckage was carried downstream and crashed against the Denver and Rio Grande Railroad bridge, known as bridge no. 110-B, weakening it and setting the stage for the "Tragedy at Eden."

At 8:20 p.m. locomotive 1009 entered bridge 110-B. As soon as the locomotive was completely on the bridge, the timbers began cracking. The engine swayed. The bridge broke, and ninety-seven lives were lost. This Missouri Pacific train wreck was the worst railroad accident to have happened in the United States at that time. A complete account of the wreck is given in Dow Helmers's Tragedy at Eden. *Photograph courtesy of the Pueblo Library District*

Working Men, Who Supported the 1901 Movement to close gambling in Pueblo

In 1905 Dr. Abraham Lincoln Fugard, while serving as coroner, led the final movement to close public gambling in Pueblo. Under the law of Colorado, the duties of sheriff fell upon the coroner when "for any reason the sheriff was unable or failed to perform his duties."

The movement to end public gambling had begun in 1901 during the second term of Mayor West. The Law and Order League wanted saloons closed on Sundays and at midnight other nights. All gambling was to stop, including cards, slot machines, roulette, and a form of gambling known as policy shops. Mayor West was an active member of the league, and under his direction an ordinance was passed on August 30, 1901, that forbade public gambling. Three months later on November 30 gambling resumed at the Greenlight and the Oriental Gambling House. Both the mayor and the police chief refused to answer reporters' questions. George B. West died before the issue was resolved. It was four more years before public gambling was successfully stopped under the direction of Dr. Fugard.

In addition to the attempt to end gambling, the first paving of streets in Pueblo commenced May 8, 1906, during the term of Mayor John T. West. Photograph courtesy of the Pueblo Library District

143

**Buildings along Main Street
Reflecting a Prosperous Town**

In 1908 a movement had begun to change Pueblo's form of government. Charles A. Ballrich was the first to suggest a commission form or system of government. For obvious reasons the politicians of all parties fought the proposition from start to finish. Court proceedings were held. Judge J. E. Rizer decided that the adoption of a charter form of government was legal. For one year the city council delayed action by failing to appropriate funds for the holding of an election.

Finally in January 1911 a special election was held. The opponents of the charter won. The pro-charter forces regrouped and began the battle again. In a spring election in 1911 the charter won by a vote of four to one. The Commerce

Club, the forerunner of the Pueblo Chamber of Commerce, assisted in the selection of candidates for the charter convention. Twenty-one delegates representing all interests were nominated and elected. The convention then formulated a charter for the city of Pueblo. The charter provided for initiative and referendum and recall; a civil service commission that made all appointments; five commissioners elected directly by the people; and the placing of city affairs on a cash basis. No wards were recognized under the provision of the charter. The city was administered as a unit.

The charter form of government began on November 20, 1911. The new city commissioners of Pueblo were Thomas D.

Donnelly, president of the council and commissioner of public safety; Victor I. Prevost, commissioner of health, inspection, and sanitation; Thomas A. Duke, commissioner of parks, lighting, and water; J. Knox Burton, commissioner of finances and supplies; and Charles A. Landon, commissioner of highways.

John T. West, who had been elected mayor at the traditional municipal elections in April 1911, was Pueblo's last mayor. The president of the city commissioners assumed the duties of mayor. Photograph courtesy of the Pueblo Library District

Theodore E. Roosevelt at the Dedication of the YMCA, 1910

The first attempt to begin a YMCA in Pueblo was in 1882. The present YMCA was organized on February 17, 1889. When it was nine days old, it had raised $4,000 and had 111 members. Former governor Alva Adams addressed the organizational meeting. Rooms in a building at Fourth and Main streets were donated by O. H. P. Baxter. During 1891 a building fund was started, and on January 13, 1894, the association entered new quarters in Pioneer Block at 117-119 South Union Avenue. In 1900 the YMCA moved to 171 North Union Avenue.

On April 14, 1909, George E. King and Mahlon D. Thatcher, Jr., were elected chairman and secretary-treasurer, respectively, of the committee to raise $100,000 for a new building. On July 6, 1910, General Thomas J. Downen, who had donated the land at 112 Eighth Street, threw in the first shovel of dirt. Former President Theodore E. Roosevelt laid the cornerstone of the new building on August 30, 1910. The building was opened to members June 1, 1915, free from debt.

On February 17, 1964, a drive was announced to secure funds for a new building. Unfortunately the drive fell short of its goal, and the board decided to construct the building in phases. The first phase was completed by December 1968.

In April 1972 Francis E. King and Mahlon T. White, the son and grandson respectively of the co-chairmen who had headed the successful drive in 1909, were appointed chairmen of a $750,000 expansion fund drive. David Packard, a native Puebloan, gave $400,000 and boosted the building fund close to its goal. The new building was dedicated October 13, 1974. Photograph courtesy of Pueblo Library District

Architect's Drawing for the Vail Hotel on Grand Avenue, 1910

The Vail Hotel, built in 1910-11, was designed by three architects, J. M. Gile of Pueblo, Robert S. Willison of Denver, and Montana S. Fallis of Denver.

John E. Vail, for whom the hotel is named, was the founder of the Star-Journal Publishing Company, which was located next door to the hotel. He helped organize and served as the chairman of the board of the Vail Hotel Company. The 300 local stockholders were particularly proud of the fine dining room and the staff of black waiters. Photograph courtesy of the Pueblo Library District

Rock Island Train Wreck

On July 30, 1912, a Rock Island passenger train traveling on Denver and Rio Grande track went into the flooded Fountain River. The conductor had not had time to check tickets and the number of passengers on the train is unknown. Several lives were lost. Photograph courtesy of the Pueblo Library District

Pueblo County Courthouse

The present Pueblo County Courthouse, at Tenth and Main streets, was completed in 1912. It is built of Turkey Creek sandstone and pink Beulah marble. Charles Schnorr painted the interior murals. Illustration courtesy of the Pueblo Library District

Stonecutters who Built the County Courthouse

Italian stone carvers crafted the neo-classical columns. One mistake would have been disastrous. Each morning the contractor purchased beer mixed with a little whiskey to help steady their hands. Photograph courtesy of the Pueblo Library District

Pueblo Fire Department Chief Sam Christy In Front of the Colorado Mineral Palace, Circa 1912

By 1912 the members of the Pueblo Fire Department had grown to fifty-one men.

The positions included chief, assistant chief, machinist, stoker, nine captains, and the firemen. The changes the department was undergoing were reflected in the equipment. The chief had both a buggy and an automobile. In addition to the six hose companies, there were one truck, two engines, one chemical unit, twenty horses, and 15,000 feet of hose. Photograph courtesy of the Pueblo Library District

Jim Flynn and Son

The man in white behind the boxers was Jim Flynn, "Pueblo's Fighting Fireman." The boy in black was Flynn's son. The peak of Flynn's career was the July 1912 bout with Jack Johnson for the heavyweight championship of the world. Flynn lost. Photograph courtesy of Gladys Hassey

148

Hartley O. Baker

Dr. Hartley O. Baker, a successful Denver physician and surgeon, moved to Pueblo in 1917 with plans to manufacture a steam automobile. Dr. Baker had used a steam automobile for making his professional calls and was aware of the shortcomings of the steam generators and boilers then in use. His perfected generator and boiler were declared by the eminent engineers of the era to be the finest available. Photograph courtesy of the Pueblo Library District

The Baker Steamer

The Baker Steamer was one of the 125 different makes of steam-powered automobiles produced in the United States. The factory, located on West Twenty-ninth Street and Baker Lane in northwest Pueblo, completed the first unit June 4, 1918. A body built by the Chandler Car Company was used. A bus, a truck, a tractor, and a few cars were made, plus many replacements for the famous Stanley Steamers' boiler-generators. The company vanished about 1921. Photograph courtesy of the Pueblo Library District

Seven Passenger Baker Steamer

Soldiers From Pueblo

Pueblo men pose before going to France to join the Pueblo unit in World War I—the war to end all wars. Photograph courtesy of the Pueblo Library District

149

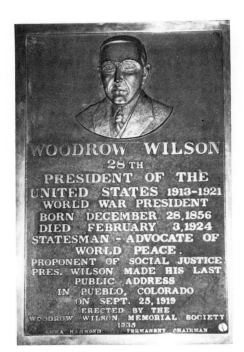

Woodrow Wilson Plaque in City Hall

President Woodrow Wilson made his last public address at the Pueblo Memorial Hall, September 25, 1919. President Wilson was traveling across the United States urging the American people to support his version of the League of Nations. Symptoms of Wilson's impending collapse appeared before he reached Pueblo. On the same day, he had spoken at the Denver City Auditorium and then traveled by train to Pueblo. He lunched on the train and upon arriving in Pueblo rode in an open car to the fairgrounds. Exhausted, the president declined to address the crowd at the fairgrounds; however, he did agree to be driven in an open car in front of the grandstands. Captain Jack Sinclair's Cowboy Band played the national anthem, cannons were fired, and everyone stood, cheered, and waved. A little after three o'clock Wilson spoke at Memorial Hall. His voice was weak. Once back on the train President Wilson's condition worsened. The remainder of his tour was canceled, and a short time later he was disabled with a stroke. He served the remaining eighteen months of his term as an invalid. The Pueblo address was his last public speech. A plaque in memorial of Woodrow Wilson's last speech is in city hall. Photograph courtesy of John E. Smith

A Ku Klux Klan Funeral at Roselawn Cemetery, 1920s

During the 1920s the Ku Klux Klan had a large Colorado membership. For many it was a social organization, complete with a drum and bugle corps. All of the reasons the Klan prospered will never be known; however, oral interviews have indicated that part of the appeal of the Klan was the fear of competition from primarily third-generation immigrants who were joining the middle class business world. Photograph courtesy of the Pueblo Library District

The Cowboy Band

Captain Jack Sinclair, night captain of the Pueblo police, was the leader of the famous Pueblo Cowboy Band. Composed of local musicians dressed in chaps and cowboy hats, the band toured America and Europe. Photograph courtesy of the Pueblo Library District

Steelworks YMCA

The five-story Steelworks YMCA in Pueblo, completed in 1920, was located on Jones Avenue between Abriendo and Evans avenues. It was the largest industrial YMCA in the world. Photograph courtesy of Gladys Hassey

Interior of the Steelworks YMCA

The Steelworks YMCA had a 1,200-seat auditorium, swimming pool, gymnasium, bowling alley, library, restaurant, ballroom, and dormitories. The building was demolished in 1963. Photograph courtesy of the Pueblo Library District

Arapahoe Grocery

The interior of the Arapahoe Grocery, 727 North Main Street, looked like this in the 1920s. Photograph courtesy of the Pueblo Library District

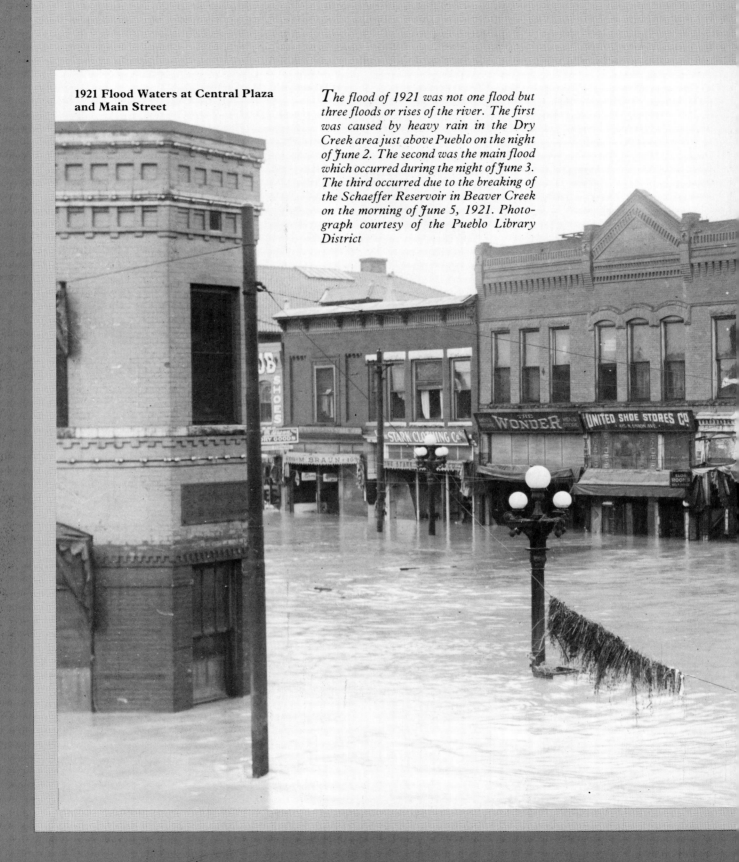

1921 Flood Waters at Central Plaza and Main Street

The flood of 1921 was not one flood but three floods or rises of the river. The first was caused by heavy rain in the Dry Creek area just above Pueblo on the night of June 2. The second was the main flood which occurred during the night of June 3. The third occurred due to the breaking of the Schaeffer Reservoir in Beaver Creek on the morning of June 5, 1921. Photograph courtesy of the Pueblo Library District

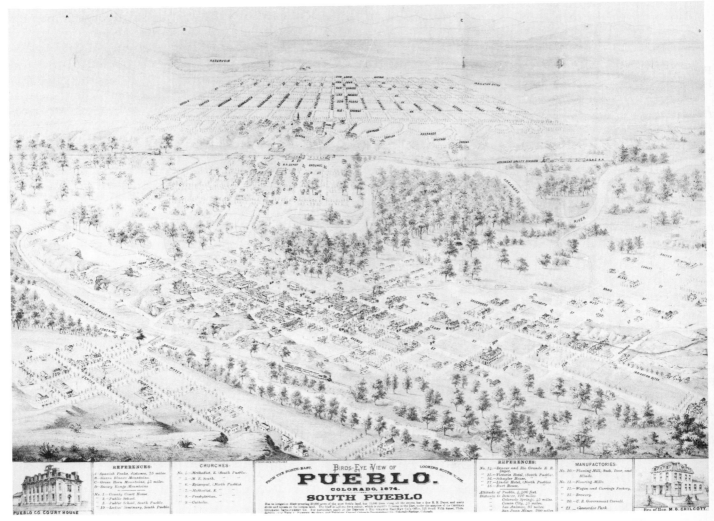

REFERENCES:

CHURCHES:

BIRDS-EYE VIEW OF
PUEBLO.
COLORADO, 1874.
SOUTH PUEBLO

REFERENCES:

MANUFACTORIES:

PUEBLO CO. COURT HOUSE

Res of Hon M. B. CHILCOTT

Pueblo, 1874

This 1874 map of Pueblo charts the meandering flow of the Arkansas River through town. Over the years the river was rechanneled repeatedly. During the 1921 flood the river returned to its original course, which explains why one building was left standing while the one next to it was washed away. Photograph courtesy of the Pueblo Library District

Flood Waters at the Union Depot During the Flood of 1921

High water marks on the buildings document a rise of the Arkansas River that seems impossible. The exact flow will never be known. The river gauges were washed away, and only estimates can be made. Pueblo Conservancy District engineers estimated the peak flow of the Arkansas in Pueblo at 100,000 cubic feet per second. At the Union Depot the high water mark was at eleven feet. At Memorial Hall it reached nine feet. The high water mark at the waterworks pump building at Fourth Street and Grand Avenue was eleven feet, eight inches. Photograph courtesy of the Pueblo Library District

154

First and Main Streets During the Flood

For twenty-seven years the levee held. Perhaps that is why people did not heed the curfew sirens that blew to warn of the approaching flood. To the young the sirens represented something to go and see. By the time the flood was in full force family members were stranded on opposite sides of town and lives had been needlessly lost. An early Bureau of Reclamation report listed 120 known deaths, 49 persons missing, and 93 not accounted for. According to the health department 88 bodies were recovered. The exact total will never be known.

Note the high water mark on what is currently the Leach Building. Photograph courtesy of the Pueblo Library District

First and Main Streets After the Flood

Twenty-five horses were drowned at the Model Dairy barn. After the flood of 1921 horses were seldom seen in the downtown area. The livery stables had been destroyed by the flood and were not rebuilt. Photograph courtesy of the Pueblo Library District

The flood of 1921 was the single most important event in the history of Pueblo. Unlike the Chicago fire which burned homes but left the business district intact, the 1921 flood destroyed Pueblo's business and industrial district.

Pueblo had survived a series of floods over the years. The floods in 1893 and 1894 had flooded the lower levels of City Hall, destroying early city records. Following each flood corrective measures had been taken. By the 1900s the levee system met the highest standards of the times. No one could have predicted that a cloudburst of the magnitude of June 1921 would occur. It did, and Pueblo's history was changed.

The Railroad Yards Near the Union Depot

The entire Arkansas River Valley, from Florence to the Kansas border, experienced flooding. The greatest damage was done in Pueblo, the chief city in the valley. Below Pueblo the loss was chiefly agricultural with more than 57,000 acres inundated, of which 4,700 acres were agricultural. The headgates of practically every irrigation system in the valley were destroyed or damaged. Photograph courtesy of the Pueblo Library District

The Aftermath of the Flood Near Union and Santa Fe Avenues

Boats from Lake Clara at Colorado Mineral Palace were used to rescue people during the early stages of the flood. People were trapped inside buildings throughout town. Burning, floating lumber, ignited by the combination of floodwater and lime at the King lumberyard, illuminated the floating chaos that engulfed Pueblo. Photograph courtesy of the Pueblo Library District

Damaged Railroad Bridge Along the Arkansas River, 1921

It was between 8 and 9 p.m. when the Arkansas began to exceed the boundaries of the levee. Later the same night Fountain Creek reached flood proportions, washing out a series of bridges. The eastern portions of the First Street and Fourth Street bridges were washed out. The Eighth Street bridge was destroyed, and a part of the railroad bridge near Third Street was washed away. Photograph courtesy of the Pueblo Library District

The Remains of What Was a Home in the Grove

The flood cut off all power, telephone service, and water pressure. Warnings to boil the drinking water were issued. Photograph courtesy of the Pueblo Library District

Pryor's Furniture Store, 127-129 North Main Street

Sheriff Sam Thomas swore in 1,500 deputies to guard the city against looters. Governor Oliver H. Shoup declared martial law. Recovery had begun. Photograph courtesy of the Pueblo Library District

Union Avenue After the Flood

Can you imagine the task of cleaning up the debris from the flood without trucks? For fifty-one days the army provided men and heavy equipment to assist in the cleanup work. According to John A. Martin, the military put "order and system into the chaos." Photograph courtesy of the Pueblo Library District

Union Depot Yards After the Flood

After the army left, Puebloans continued with the cleanup work. Photograph courtesy of the Pueblo Library District

Puebloans salvaging all that they could.

Photograph courtesy of the Pueblo Library District

Josephine Pryor, One of the Heroines of the Flood

Recovery was hampered by the loss of telephone service. By late June service had been restored to most of the city, with the exception of the portion of the city most damaged by the flood. When telephone service was restored, Puebloans used their phones with a new appreciation.

Thousands of lives had been saved by the Mountain State Telephone and Telegraph Company staff. When the flood sirens began, off-duty staff members returned to the office located on D Street between Union and Victoria avenues and began warning people. All of the staff stayed at their posts until the lines went down. Then it was too late to escape from the building. The thirteen staff members stayed on the second floor and waited for the flood to recede. They were Josephine Pryor, chief operator, Mathilda M. Anderson, Georgia A. Armstrong, Roscoe D. Atterberry, John F. Elliott, Ward P. Gammons, Carl E. Garnett, Julia A. Moynihan,

Ethel D. Richards, Julia A. Swanson, Margaret Williams, Alexander W. Young, and the man who saved the business records, Byron Thady. Photograph courtesy of the Pueblo Library District

Flood Debris in the Alley of 300 West Ninth Street

Pueblo, with an assessed valuation of $33 million, suffered losses that were estimated from $10 million to $19 million, or from one-third to two-thirds of the economic base of the city. Railroad companies, businessmen, and property owners bore the economic burden alone. The only government assistance of any consequence was an appropriation by Congress of $100,000 to assist the army in cleanup work. Photograph courtesy of the Pueblo Library District

**St. Michael's Eastern Orthodox
Church, 816 East B Street**

*In addition to the loss of life, property,
and many small businesses, Pueblo lost a
portion of her architectural heritage in
the 1921 flood. Along the southern portion
of Santa Fe Avenue, in the Grove, and
along the banks of both rivers the earliest
dwellings and buildings had been erected.
These wooden and adobe buildings were
Pueblo's frontier architecture and they
were lost.*

*St. Michael's was moved from the
Grove to 801 West Summit Avenue. The
dome was salvaged and added to the new
church. Photograph courtesy of the Pueblo
Library District*

The Vincenzo Laurino Grocery, 181 South Santa Fe Avenue, the Building at the End of the Road

For years Puebloans fought the financing of the Moffat Tunnel. Railroaders knew the shorter route through the mountains would take traffic away from Pueblo. The flood of 1921 forced a compromise between northern and southern Colorado. On April 8, 1922, Governor Oliver Shoup called a special session of the state legislature. On that day bills were passed which provided for the creation of and funding for the Moffat Tunnel Commission and the Pueblo Conservancy District. Pueblo would lose a portion of Colorado's railroad business, but the Arkansas River would be rechanneled and a dam built. Photograph courtesy of the Pueblo Library District

Cardillo Family Home

This picture of the home of the Cardillo family in the 100 block of Santa Fe Avenue is one of the few photographs of the housing along Santa Fe Avenue before the 1921 flood. Pueblo's first structures were wood and were probably built along the same patterns. Photograph courtesy of the Pueblo Library District

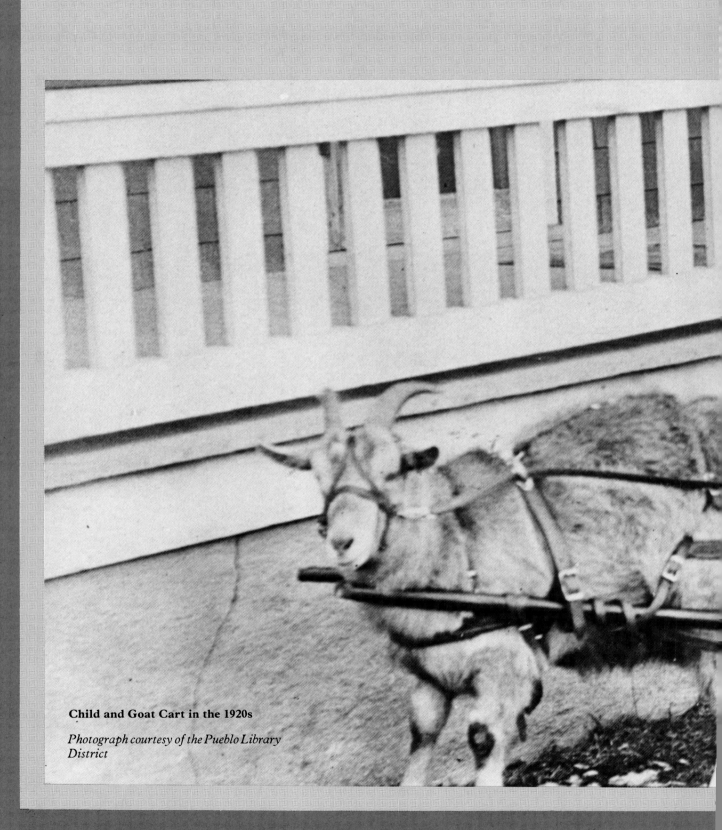

Child and Goat Cart in the 1920s

Photograph courtesy of the Pueblo Library District

Chapter Nine
Drought, Depression, and Recovery

Mid-Continent Air Express, Providing Air Mail Service for Pueblo in 1925

The Pueblo Airport was located along what is now Prairie Avenue. Photograph courtesy of the Pueblo Library District

Soldiers and Sailors of the World War

The Solider and Sailors of the World War marker was dedicted by the Daughters of the American Revolution, March 6, 1927. Originally located in the Greenwood Parkway, the marker is now located to the west of city hall. The DAR has been responsible for the erection of most of the historical markers in Pueblo County. Photograph courtesy of the Pueblo Library District

Boom and bust have been Pueblo's companions from the beginning. Financial panic was followed by financial panic. The crash in 1929 failed to bring a rush of new problems because Pueblo's economy was already in trouble. Agriculture had been economically depressed since the end of World War I. War-inflated grain and livestock prices fell 60 percent within three years. Many of Pueblo's small industries had not reopened after the 1921 flood. Completion of the Moffat tunnel reduced the railroad market. And, there was drought. For five consecutive years, 1933 to 1938, dust storms ravaged the land. Throughout the thirties and forties Pueblo County's population was becoming older. Pueblo was a mature community with serious problems. It would not be until the development of the Pueblo Army Air Base and the Pueblo Ordinance Depot during World War II that recovery would be achieved.

Reverend Charles J. Murray, S. J. at the Dedication of the Salt Creek Community Building, Circa 1942

One of Pueblo's oldest neighborhoods, Salt Creek, began in the 1870s, and is probably named for the small stream that runs through the area on its west side. Before the smelters and the steelworks existed, Hispanic families had settled the area. Over the years others acquired title to the land, and Hispanics became squatters.

In 1942 Father Murray, then assistant pastor of Mount Carmel, and a small group of parishioners organized Mount Carmel Credit Union. Business began in January 1943 in the basement of Mount Carmel Church. The first major goal of the credit union was to assist the squatters in Smelter Hill, Pepper Sauce Bottoms, and Salt Creek to obtain title to their homes. Photograph courtesy of the Pueblo Library District

165

**Salt Creek's Sagrada Familia
Catholic Chapel, Circa 1920**

In the heart of Salt Creek, east of Pueblo, the Mount Carmel Credit Union helped a colony of squatters to acquire legal title to their land. Justice William S. Jackson of the Colorado Supreme Court owned the land. The credit union induced him to sell the property to it so it could be subdivided properly and sold to the occupants. Included in the plot was the Sagrada Familia ("Holy Family") Catholic Chapel, built there prior to 1900.

Twenty squatters in Pepper Sauce Bottoms were able to obtain legal title to their homes with the credit union's assistance. The area, now legally known as the Bronx, is adjacent to the Santa Fe Railroad yards.

Smelter Hill, now known as Toledo Heights, had sixty-four adobe homes, built early in the century by emigrants from Mexico who found jobs in the nearby

smelter. A man used to come around once a month and collect rent for the land. The land had belonged to the defunct Jackson-Carlile Land Company. No one had paid taxes on the land for many years. Matters became serious when a Puebloan bought up the tax titles to the land and demanded that the squatters pay rent or else vacate the buildings. Mount Carmel Credit Union obtained quitclaims from the defunct land company and redeemed the tax certificates. The area was surveyed and subdivided. The survey followed the existing fences so that the families would not be disturbed.

As these people reimbursed the credit union for the expense involved, they received valid deeds for the properties. The cost ranged from $35 to $110. Photograph courtesy of the Pueblo Library District

166

Pueblo County Farm, Twentieth Lane and County Farm Road, Circa 1930

The Pueblo County Farm, located on the corner of Twentieth Lane and County Farm Road, was a home for indigent residents of Pueblo County. Those who were able worked on the farm. In 1930 the farm produced milk, butterfat, corn, hay, chickens, eggs, green beans, onions, cabbage, carrots, parsnips, turnips, beets, apples, calves, pigs, pumpkins, lettuce, radishes, melons, and cauliflower. Photograph courtesy of the Pueblo Library District

From 1923 to 1937 prolonged drought and high winds caused tremendous damage through soil erosion.

Photograph courtesy of the Pueblo Library District

The 1965 Drought/Wind Damage Was Similiar to That of the 1930s

One Beulah resident recalled that they dragged a chain behind the car when they drove into Pueblo during the Dust Bowl era to prevent static electricity from harming the battery. Photograph courtesy of David Roscover

Dust Masks

Grace Chason, Vallie Ballas, and Olga Ballas of the Harding Bullock's Store on Main Street advertise the three models of dust masks that were available at the store circa 1930. Photograph courtesy of the Pueblo Library District

An Unidentified Man Advertising a Movie at the Main Theatre, Circa 1932

In 1929 the Depression hit with the stock market crash on Wall Street. Many Puebloans remember helping others as they moved from place to place in search of employment. Photograph courtesy of the Pueblo Library District

Temporary Shelter for an Unemployed Puebloan, Circa 1932

By 1932 the Depression had deepened and unemployment increased.
Farm prices had dropped to rock bottom. Hogs sold for three dollars per 100 pounds, eggs sold for ten cents a dozen, and wheat sold for fifty cents a bushel. Photograph courtesy of the Pueblo Library District

**The Colorado Fuel and Iron Company
Wire Mill, Circa 1935**

*In 1933 the Colorado Fuel and Iron
Company went into receivership under the
bankruptcy laws. The company was reor-
ganized in 1936 as the Colorado Fuel and
Iron Corporation. The presidents were
Arthur Roeder, 1936-38; W. A. Maxwell,
Jr., 1938-45; E. P. Holder, 1945-46;
C. W. Meyers, 1946-52, A. F. Franz,
1952-61; Leonard C. Rose, 1961-65;
and Rudolph Smith, 1965-66. Photo-
graph courtesy of the Pueblo Library
District*

Entrance to the Colorado State Hospital, 1930s

The Colorado State Hospital faced difficult times during the 1920s and 1930s. The patient load increased while the funding decreased. The young men and women who had come during the mining booms were becoming old and unable to care for themselves. Returning patients to their home regions was one way of coping. By 1925 Colorado had been a state for only forty-nine years. The patients admitted during 1925-26 included 25 from Germany, 17 from England, 13 from Austria, 16 from Italy, 22 from Mexico, 14 from Russia, 18 from Sweden, 46 from Illinois, 37 from Kansas, 34 from Iowa, 61 from Missouri, and 103 from Colorado.

A special appropriation was received to deport eighteen nonresident patients to the states or foreign countries in which they had residence. Prior to the special appropriations the hospital had paid for the transportation from the operating budget. Photograph courtesy of the Pueblo Library District

Colorado State Hospital Woodcroft Annex Flood, 1935

The Woodcroft Hospital was purchased to provide additional accommodations as the Colorado State Hospital Annex.

The Fountain River flooded the Colorado State Hospital annex at Twenty-ninth and Court on Decoration Day, 1935. A ward building and four employees' cottages were swept away. On August 6, 1936, the Fountain River again flooded the annex and took two more employees' cottages and so much of the grounds that the remaining ward buildings were endangered.

Today the Pueblo Mall occupies the former site of the Woodcroft Hospital. Later the hospital moved to Abriendo Avenue. The Sharmar Nursing Center currently operates on the hospital site. Photograph courtesy of the Pueblo Library District

Aerial View of the Colorado State Hospital, 1940-41

Over 113 separate projects were completed in the 1930s by the Works Progress Administration for the state hospital. Facilities for the care and treatment of nearly 1,200 patients were added. All new structures were of stone obtained *from a quarry leased by the hospital. The recreation building is in the middle, and the Female Center is in the foreground. Photograph courtesy of the Pueblo Library District*

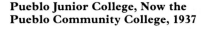

Pueblo Junior College, Now the Pueblo Community College, 1937

Pueblo Junior College was created June 28, 1933. The first classes were held on the top floor of the Pueblo County Courthouse. By fall 1937 the first of the Works Progress Administration buildings for the West Orman Avenue campus had been completed, and the school moved from the courthouse to the campus. In 1961 the Colorado General Assembly *enacted legislation which made Pueblo Junior College a four-year institution, known as Southern Colorado State College (SCSC).*

Work began in 1964 on the first buildings on the new Belmont campus. The college became the University of Southern Colorado on July 1, 1975. In 1979 the vocational school was separated from the *university by state legislative mandate and became Pueblo Vocational Community College. Today known as Pueblo Community College, it is located on the original site of Pueblo Junior College. Photograph courtesy of the Pueblo Library District*

YWCA, 801 North Santa Fe Avenue, 1940s

The Pueblo YWCA was begun in 1914 and incorporated in 1916 to serve the interests of young working women. Its first location was at 219 West Third Street, where it offered a three-story residence hall and cafeteria. This location was devastated in the flood of 1921. In August 1922 the YWCA moved to the old Frederick Heller estate at Eighth Street and Santa Fe Avenue. In 1923 the

YWCA became a participating agency of the Community Chest, forerunner of United Way. A drive for a new building was initiated in 1930, a contract let in 1934, and the present building occupied in 1935. In 1980, the YWCA building was placed on the National Register of Historic Places. Photograph courtesy of the Pueblo Library District

**An Early Phillips Boy's Band,
Circa 1930**

*D. Z. Phillips Music Store at 621
North Main Street sponsored the Phillips'
Boys Band, later known as the Phillips
Crusaders Boys' Military Band. Open to
boys ages eight to fourteen, the band's
slogan was "Building boys is better than
mending men." By 1945 there were over
100 members of the band. Photograph
courtesy of the Pueblo Library District*

Phillips' Highland Lassies was an all-girls band in the 1940s.

Phillips' Highland Lassies was an all-girls band in the 1940s. Photograph courtesy of the Pueblo Library District

**President Franklin D. Roosevelt
giving one of his train platform
speeches at the Pueblo Union Depot
in 1938**

*Photograph courtesy of the Pueblo Library
District*

**The Pueblo Country Club, 3200
Eighth Avenue, Circa 1938**

*Photograph courtesy of the Pueblo Library
District*

176

**Pueblo Mountain Park, Beulah,
Colorado, May 19, 1938**

*Pueblo has a tradition of fine parks.
Pueblo Mountain Park, which is the
largest city park, consists of 611 acres
developed by the Works Progress Administration circa 1938 in Beulah. The Mineral
Palace Park houses the city greenhouse
and Lake Clara, named for Clara Noble.
The City Park includes the Pueblo
Zoological Gardens, tennis courts, summer
amusement rides for children, a lake, and
access to the popular bike trails system on
its 161.25 acres. Some of the other Pueblo
parks are Minnequa Park, Fairmont
Park, Bradford Park, Mitchell Park,
and Royal Park, named in honor of
Andrew Royal. Photograph courtesy of
the Pueblo Library District*

Governor Teller Ammons, son of former Governor Elias Ammons, at the Colorado State Fair, Circa 1938.

Photograph courtesy of the Pueblo Library District

Jonnie Grimes and His Famous Brahma Bull New Deal, at the Colorado State Fair, Circa 1938

Photograph courtesy of the Pueblo Library District

Little Tin Horn Hank, a Rope Artist

Photograph courtesy of the Pueblo Library District

Rose Herlin on Dare Devil at the Colorado State Fair, Circa 1938

Photograph courtesy of the Pueblo Library District

Ray and Marvin Ramsey performing the four-horse Roman Jump at the Colorado State Fair, Circa 1938

Photograph courtesy of the Pueblo Library District

Pueblo Army Depot, Circa 1965

In 1941 the site for what was to become the Pueblo Ordnance Depot was selected when national defense was accelerated prior to the entry of the United States into World War II. The acquisition of the land in 1942 was completed under the First War Powers Act of 1941 and Executive Order 9001. Responsibility for the depot was assumed by the Army Ordnance Corps in April 1942, and the first group of civilians was hired. In August the first carload of ammunition was received for storage.

After the war the depot served as a six-state ammunition distribution center, provided maintenance for several of the missile programs, and in 1962 was renamed the Pueblo Army Depot. In 1971 the depot was named as a repository for the United States Army historical properties. In 1972 the German war art collection arrived. Today the depot is known as the Pueblo Depot Activity. Photograph courtesy of the United States Army

Italian Prisoners of War Working at the Depot, Circa 1944

In 1944 a group of Italian prisoners of war were held at the depot. They had been captured during the North African campaign. Local Italian families invited some of them for dinner, and some of the soldiers met Pueblo women, married, and remained in the United States. Photograph courtesy of the United States Army

Hotel Whitman, Main and Ninth Streets, Circa 1940

During the 1940s the Hotel Whitman was Pueblo's most popular hotel. The 150-room hotel boasted fine food correctly served and a radio in every room. Two of the best-remembered guests were Clark Gable, who visited while stationed at the Pueblo Army Air Base, and Mamie Eisenhower. Photograph courtesy of the Pueblo Library District

Pueblo Dodgers, 1955

Runyon Field, named for Damon Runyon, was the home of the Class A Western League Pueblo Dodgers from 1947 to 1958. The farm team of the Brooklyn Dodgers represented the third Western League team to play in Pueblo. Oneal M. Hobbs, the general manager, is the first man in the middle row on the right side. Photograph courtesy of the Pueblo Library District

Pueblo Memorial Airport

The training of long range, heavy bombardment crews began at the Pueblo Army Air Base in the fall of 1942. The B-24, known as the Liberator, was the plane for which most of the crews were trained. The 308th Bombardment Group, known as the Flying Tigers, trained at the base in 1942 and 1943. Today the base is the Pueblo Memorial Airport. On July 20, 1948, the city was given a quitclaim deed to the air base. On January 1, 1953, the municipal airport was moved to the air base, and on August 1, 1954, the administration building was dedicated and the base was renamed the Pueblo Memorial Airport in memory of the veterans of World War II. Photograph by Edwin L. Dodds

The *Star-Journal* and *Chieftain* building at 825 West Sixth Street, completed in February 1961

Photograph by Edwin L. Dodds

Pueblo Library District's McClelland Library, 100 East Abriendo Avenue

On June 1, 1965, the new library building, the McClelland Public Library, opened for circulation. In 1945 the service of the library had been extended to Pueblo County when the county commissioners began making annual appropriations to supplement city funds. By 1948 the bookmobile service was established, and in 1962 the Belmont branch opened.

On January 1, 1969, the Pueblo Regional Library District was created by joint resolution of the city of Pueblo and the board of county commissioners. This provided for a separate tax base for the library, according to Colorado law. In 1979 the Pueblo Regional Library District became the Pueblo Library District in accordance with state regulations regarding the use of the word regional in a library's name. Photograph by Edwin L. Dodds

The CF&I Steel Corporation Offices, 1982

In 1966 the company's name was changed to CF&I Steel Corporation. The presidents were Frederick A. Fielder, 1966-70; C. Clay Crawford, 1970-76; Robert J. Slater, 1976-80; and Frank J. Yaklich, Jr., 1980 to the present. In 1969 the CF&I was acquired by Crane Company, and in 1970 Clay Crawford became the first CF&I president to be headquartered in Pueblo. Photograph by Edwin L. Dodds

President John F. Kennedy, Dutch Clark Stadium, 1962

On August 17, 1962, President John F. Kennedy spoke at the Dutch Clark Stadium on the approval of the Frying-pan-Arkansas Project. The following quotation is extracted from his remarks that day:

> *I hope that those of us who hold positions of public responsibility in 1962 are as far-seeing about the needs of the country in 1982 and 1992 as those men and women were thirty years ago who began to make this project possible. The world may have been built in seven days, but this project was built in thirty years, and it took labor, day in and day out, week in and week out, month in and month out, year in and year out, by Congressmen and Senators, and citizens, and the press of this state, to make this project possible.*

Photograph courtesy of the John F. Kennedy Library

Pueblo West in 1981

Today, Lake Pueblo serves as one of the links in this continuing water conservation program. Located adjacent to the Pueblo Dam and Reservoir (Lake Pueblo), Pueblo West was established on September 16, 1969, and encompasses 26,685 acres, a development of McCulloch Properties. White jeeps and charter flights were provided to introduce prospective residents to a new type of housing development for those who love the plains. Photograph courtesy of the Pueblo Library District

The Pueblo-Puebla Plaza, at the Former Site of the Fountain Building

The plaza is bordered by Union, Grand, and Victoria avenues. The Pueblo, Colorado, sister city program with Puebla, Mexico, began in 1970. The plaza, with the eagle metal sculpture by Jesus Coro Ferrer of Puebla, was dedicated August 25, 1973. Photograph by Edwin L. Dodds

**View of Pueblo Commercial District
as seen from the Blocks, the Arkansas
River Channel in the Foreground**

Photograph by Edwin L. Dodds

**Pueblo Chamber of Commerce,
Third Street and Santa Fe Avenue**

*Through the years, the Pueblo Chamber
of Commerce has had many homes, but in
1970 the organization moved into its new
handsome quarters at Third Street and
Santa Fe Avenue, next to the Sangre de
Cristo Arts and Conference Center. The
chamber presently has about 1,000
members and serves as the voice of business
in Pueblo. Photograph by Edwin L.
Dodds*

Murals by University of Southern Colorado Art Students

Photograph by Edwin L. Dodds

Nineteen eighty-six will mark the 100th anniversary of the consolidation of Pueblo. Identified by many as a working class community, Puebloans have a no nonsense view of the world. Traditional values are honored as is the opportunity to be oneself. Puebloans know and love their community and look forward to their future.

Pueblo City Hall and Memorial Hall

These structures were built by the same contractor, C. S. Lambie Company, but were designed by different architects. City Hall, built in 1917, was designed by W. E. Stickney. Memorial Hall, named in honor of those who lost their lives in World War I, was designed by Godley and Haskey and built in 1919. Photograph by Edwin L. Dodds

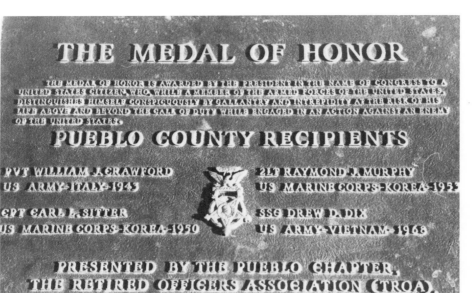

THE MEDAL OF HONOR

THE MEDAL OF HONOR IS AWARDED BY THE PRESIDENT IN THE NAME OF CONGRESS TO A UNITED STATES CITIZEN, WHO, WHILE A MEMBER OF THE ARMED FORCES OF THE UNITED STATES, DISTINGUISHES HIMSELF CONSPICUOUSLY BY GALLANTRY AND INTREPIDITY AT THE RISK OF HIS LIFE ABOVE AND BEYOND THE CALL OF DUTY WHILE ENGAGED IN AN ACTION AGAINST AN ENEMY OF THE UNITED STATES.

PUEBLO COUNTY RECIPIENTS

PVT WILLIAM J. CRAWFORD
US ARMY-ITALY-1943

2LT RAYMOND J. MURPHY
US MARINE CORPS-KOREA-1953

CPT CARL L. SITTER
US MARINE CORPS-KOREA-1950

SSG DREW D. DIX
US ARMY-VIETNAM-1968

PRESENTED BY THE PUEBLO CHAPTER,
THE RETIRED OFFICERS ASSOCIATION (TROA),
NOVEMBER 11, 1976

The Medal of Honor Plaque at City Hall

*T*he Congressional Medal of Honor has been awarded to four men from Pueblo. Two of the recipients served in the United States Army and two served in the United States Marine Corps. One was for service in World War II, two for the Korean, and one for the Vietnam War. Although most medals of honor are awarded posthumously, all four Pueblo men survived the action. They are Drew D. Dix, Sergeant United States Army, Vietnam War; Raymond "Jerry" J. Murphy, Second Lieutenant United States Marine Corps, Korean War; Carl L. Sitter, Captain United States Marine Corps, Korean War; and William J. Crawford, Private United States Army, World War II. Photograph by John E. Smith

Historical Plaque at City Hall

*T*hree ships in the United States Navy have been named for the city and county of Pueblo, Colorado. The first Pueblo, built as the U.S.S. Colorado (armoured cruiser 7), served under the latter name until renamed U.S.S. Pueblo November 9, 1916. The second Pueblo, commissioned May 27, 1944, was a weather tracking ship with the Western Sea Frontier. She was decommissioned April 6, 1946, after serving on both the west and east coasts.

The third Pueblo, built for the Army Transportation Corps, was launched April 16, 1944. The supply vessel served in the Philippines as an army harbor craft. She was taken out of service in 1954. No longer needed by the army, she was transferred to the navy April 12, 1966, and renamed Pueblo on June 16, 1966. She was converted to an environmental research vessel and redesignated AGER-2 May 2, 1967, with Commander Lloyd M. Bucher in command. Pueblo was assigned to intelligence and oceanographic data collection in the Sea of Japan.

On January 23, 1968, while in international waters, the ship was closed on by a North Korean patrol boat and ordered to leave the area or be fired upon. U.S.S. Pueblo continued. Additional patrol craft later joined the first, and, after firing on U.S.S. Pueblo and wounding four of her crew, boarded the ship and took her to Wonsan Harbor. Her eighty surviving crew members and two civilian oceanographers, held captive eleven months, were released at Panmunjon on December 23, 1968. Photograph courtesy of John E. Smith

**The Third Pueblo County
Courthouse at Tenth and Main
Streets**

*The courthouse, which occupies an entire
block, is faced with Turkey Creek white
sandstone over brick walls two feet thick.
The stone was cut and dressed at Stone
City, Colorado. Albert R. Ross of New
York was the architect. Frank Taylor
was the contractor, and George Roe, a
Pueblo architect, was the superintendent
of construction.*

*A series of murals, painted in 1917, by
J. Charles Schnoor depicts the cattle
trade, manufacturing, and industry. The
pictures in the former courtrooms are of
Kit Carson, Alan Bradford, G. M. Chilcott, Harley Sanderson, Steven Smith,
and Henry Thatcher. The courthouse, on
the National Register of Historic Places,
was commissioned in 1908 and completed
in 1912. Photograph by Edwin L. Dodds*

**The Pueblo Federal Building,
Located on the Corner of Fifth and
Main Streets, completed in 1897**

*William Aiken, who contributed much to
the improvement of federal government
architecture throughout the United States,
was the architect. The Pueblo Federal
Building has housed a number of govern-
mental services including the United States
Post Office, Land Office, Marshal and
Weather Bureau.*

*The Pueblo Federal Building is on the
National Register of Historic Places.
Photograph by Edwin L. Dodds*

The Pueblo YMCA, 215 East Seventh Street

Dedicated October 13, 1974, the YMCA is now a family organization with emphasis on all of the family members. Photograph by Edwin L. Dodds

The Show Room, 102 South Oneida Street, Pueblo's Oldest Building

The present building was constructed in two parts. The original building was erected in 1869 by the Quaker Mills Company and was constructed from native Colorado materials. The stone walls are thirty-two inches thick and are supported and tied together with huge hand-hewn timbers from Mace's Hole or Beulah. In 1890 Julius Fist and Company built onto the front of the original building. Today the building is the property of Otterstein and Company, who converted the building into a museum and playhouse for the Impossible Players.

The Showroom is on the National Register of Historic Places. Photograph by Edwin L. Dodds

The Benevolent and Protective Order of Elks, Pueblo Lodge No. 90

The lodge was instituted Saturday, May 26, 1888. Meetings were held Sunday nights on the third floor of the Stockgrowers Bank, 227 Santa Fe Avenue. The lodge charter was completed July 12, 1890, with eighteen members. In 1904 the club purchased the former St. James Hotel, 424-426 Santa Fe Avenue, and moved in about September 30. The St. James was originally built in 1881 by Numa Vidal, a Leadville restaurateur. The architect was F. C. Eberty of Denver. The Hotel Numa became the Hotel St. James on November 1, 1881. Photograph by Edwin L. Dodds

101 North Union Avenue

Structures built in the boom era have stonework that requires careful attention to be seen. Most Puebloans are aware of these buildings on Union Avenue. However, how many know where these architectural features are located? Photographs by Edwin L. Dodds

330 South Union Avenue

226 South Union Avenue

200 South Union Avenue

101 North Union Avenue

304 South Union Avenue

Pueblo Action Incorporated now occupies what was the telephone company building during the flood of 1921.

Photograph by Edwin L. Dodds

The Christopher Columbus Monument

This monument was erected under the auspices of the Columbian Federation, October 12, 1905, by the Italians of America in honor of Columbus Day. The presiding officers were H. Chiariglione, president, C. F. Delliquardi, secretary, and M. Pagano, treasurer.

The statue is located in the 100 Block of Abriendo Avenue. Photograph by Edwin L. Dodds

A Restored Carousel Horse

The City Park carousel is a "Three Abreast" C. W. Parker "Jumping Horse Carry-Us-All," having thirty-six horses, one lovers' tub, and one chariot. The Parker factory records state that the machine was the first sold in 1911 to the Exposition and Amusement Company for $5,160.

The carousel was returned to the factory in 1914 and resold to J. J. McQuillan, owner of the Lake Minnequa Amusement Park, Pueblo, Colorado, for $3,075. The amusement park fell into decline during the Depression. During the period between Mr. McQuillan's death in 1937 and September 4, 1941, the carousel was

acquired by the city of Pueblo and moved to City Park. Currently a citizen's group is raising funds to restore the carousel horses to their original beauty. Photograph courtesy of the Pueblo Parks and Recreation Department

St. Mary Corwin Hospital, 1008 Minnequa Avenue

The hospital celebrated 100 years of service to the community in 1982. The celebration activities focused on the theme "a celebration of life." Photograph courtesy of St. Mary Corwin Hospital

Parkview Episcopal Hospital

Early in 1923 a group of physicians supported by community leaders organized a new hospital called Parkview. The doctors, H. A. Black, W. T. H. Baker, Fritz Lasser, George Myers, Carl Maynard, and Guy Hopkins, were instrumental in establishing the new facility. Their primary purpose was to establish a hospital on the north side of Pueblo and thereby provide a health care facility in which they could practice medicine. No longer would floods like the disaster of 1921 leave a large portion of the community isolated from acute care.

Parkview Episcopal Hospital opened its doors March 17, 1923, in the Wells residence at Seventeenth Street and Grand Avenue.

The 305-bed facility that exists today still occupies a portion of that property. Photograph courtesy of Parkview Episcopal Hospital

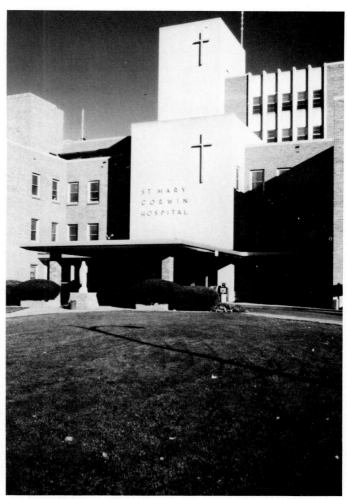

First Baptist Church of Pueblo

This church was organized in the fall of 1872. The church was incorporated October 4, 1873. Early Sunday school and church services were held in homes and storerooms near Seventh and Main streets. On June 17, 1880, the church purchased *the lots at Ninth Street and Grand Avenue. The cornerstone for the new church building was laid by Governor Pitkin in June 1, 1882. On December 9, 1962, the current educational building was dedicated. Next, the 1882 sanctuary was razed, and on May 25, 1975, the current sanctuary was dedicated. Photograph by Edwin L. Dodds*

St. Michael's Eastern Orthodox Church

The existence of a native-language church was an important factor in the selection of a new home for immigrants. The organizational meeting of St. Michael's Eastern Orthodox Church was held on June 10, 1900. The articles of incorporation were signed on July 6, 1900, and the trustees purchased *land on B and Palm streets. In 1903 construction began on the church building.*

This wooden frame building was destroyed during the June 3, 1921, flood. A new building site at 801 West Summit Avenue was selected for the brick church, with the lot donated by C.F.&I. The dome from the original building was moved to the new building. Photograph courtesy of the Pueblo Library District

The Pitkin Place Historic District, 300 Block West Pitkin Avenue, a Grouping of Seven Residences

In the early 1890s the architect/contractor team of George Roe and E. W. Shutt built six of the seven houses. The seventh was constructed in 1911. The district is on the National Register of Historic Places. Number One Pitkin Place (302 West Pitkin Avenue) was built between 1893-94 and is the most decorative Victorian-style house on the block. This was the home of Theodore W. Robinson, general superintendent of the Colorado Fuel and Iron Company's iron and steel department. Photograph by Edwin L. Dodds

Number Two Pitkin Place,
306 West Pitkin Avenue

*T*his home is characteristic of the Queen Anne style. The steep multi-gable roof is composed of differing materials—wood shingles, decorative shingles, and brick facing. The windows throughout the residence are of irregular size. This was the home of the assistant superintendent of the Colorado Fuel and Iron Company's iron and steel department, Charles Snelling Robinson, a brother of T. W. Robinson. Photograph by Edwin L. Dodds

Number Five Pitkin Place,
318 West Pitkin Avenue, Constructed
in 1895

Photograph by Edwin L. Dodds

Number Three Pitkin Place,
310 West Pitkin Avenue

*T*he outstanding design features of this house are the three-story tower on the west side, with its second-story open-air porch; the semi-elliptical stained-glass window high on the front gable; and the variety of dormer shapes dotting the roofline. Photograph by Edwin L. Dodds

Number Four Pitkin Place,
314 West Pitkin Avenue, Constructed
in 1892

Photograph by Edwin L. Dodds

Number Seven Pitkin Place,
326 West Pitkin Avenue, Home of
Attorney J. H. Mechem

*C*onstructed of stone and brick, the home has a large three-and-one-half-story tower on the east side. Number Six Pitkin Place, 322 West Pitkin Avenue, was not constructed until 1911 and is of the bungaloid style. Photograph by Edwin L. Dodds

Transportation Test Center Levitated Research Vehicle

The Transportation Test Center, located on fifty-two square miles east of Pueblo, officially opened May 19, 1971. Early tests focused on new developments in ground transportation, such as this Tracked Levitated Research Vehicle. Photograph by John L. Proffitt; courtesy of the Transportation Test Center

Train-To-Train Impact Test

This test reflects the changing research thrust towards problem solving for today's rail transportation. On October 1, 1982, the Transportation Test Center was transferred from the United States Department of Transportation to the Association of American Railroads. Photograph by Edwin L. Dodds; courtesy of the Transportation Test Center

Comanche Steam Electric Generating Station

Located on the plains southeast of Pueblo, the station was constructed from 1973 to 1975. Photograph by Edwin L. Dodds

Sangre de Cristo Arts and Conference Center

The grand opening of the center, 210 North Santa Fe Avenue, was held June 2, 1972. Proposed by the Pueblo Arts Council, the center was funded by the Pueblo County Commissioners and the U.S. Economic Development Administration. The firm of Hurtig, Gardner and Froelich were the architects. The center's program includes creative arts workshops, resident artists in dance and theater arts, a 7,000-square-foot conference center, and the Three Peaks Gift Shop. On February 22, 1980, Francis E. King, of the King Lumber Company, formally gave his Western art collection to the center. The collection will open in 1982 in the new Helen T. White Gallery. Photograph by Edwin L. Dodds

Lake Pueblo

Originally known as the Pueblo Dam and Reservoir, Lake Pueblo opened to boating and recreation on July 1, 1975. Photograph by William Hawkins, Pueblo Chieftain/Star-Journal

Pueblo Bank and Trust Building

The Pueblo Bank and Trust Company began on Union Avenue as the Pueblo Savings Bank. Incorporated at the close of 1889, the bank opened for business January 1, 1890. At that time Pueblo banks were not accepting savings accounts. Recognizing the need to provide this service, the other banks supported the directors of the newly formed bank. The directors were Alva Adams, M. D. Thatcher, W. L. Graham, J. N. Carlile, T. A. Sloan, and George J. Dunbaugh. Tradesmen, mechanics, laborers, servants, minors, and others could then receive interest on their accounts.

The location and name of the bank have undergone several changes. First located in the north room of the Bayle Building, it was moved in December 1890 to the Board of Trade Building. Next it moved to the Kretschmer Triangle Building in 1896. The bank transferred its operations to the Whitcomb Block, Third and Main streets, in 1904. The services of the bank were enlarged in 1909 and the name was changed to the Pueblo Savings and Trust Company. In 1960 the bank building (shown) was completed, and in 1963 it became the Pueblo Bank and Trust Company to properly describe it as a full-service bank. Photograph by Edwin L. Dodds

First National Bank

Pueblo's oldest bank, the First National is located in the Thatcher Building at the corner of Main and Fifth streets, where it moved April 11, 1914. Photograph by Edwin L. Dodds

United Bank of Pueblo

Formerly the Arkansas Valley Bank, the United Bank of Pueblo opened July 21, 1975, at its Eighth and Main street location. The new building was constructed during the silver anniversary of the bank. Photograph by Edwin L. Dodds

Pueblo Mall

The Pueblo Mall opened October 7, 1976. Ernest Hahn was the developer. Photograph by Edwin L. Dodds

The Pueblo School District 70 Administration Building

Located at 24951 East Highway 50, this building serves the schools of Pueblo County. In July 1950 thirty-four Pueblo County schools consolidated into one district. In 1953 the Pueblo County High School opened. Admiral Arleigh A. Burke, Chief of Naval Operations, U.S. Navy, dedicated seven new elementary schools on Saturday, March 19, 1960. He flew to each site by helicopter. The seven new schools were Baxter, Beulah, Boone, North Mesa, Rye, South Mesa, and Vineland. Photograph by Edwin L. Dodds

The Orman-Adams Residence, 102 West Orman

This house was the Pueblo School District administration building from 1952 to 1979. Placed on the National Register of Historic Places in honor of James Orman and Alva B. Adams, the building was constructed in 1890. James Orman, governor of Colorado from 1901 until 1903, occupied the house from 1891 to 1918. The residence was purchased by the Adams family in 1918.

Alva Adams, his wife, and son Alva B. Adams moved into the home that same year. Alva Adams served as governor of Colorado on three different occasions. Alva B. Adams was United States senator by appointment from 1922 to 1924. He was elected to the United States Senate in 1932 and served until his death in 1941. The building is currently the office of physicians Richard Lawrence, Donald C. Luebke, James G. Martin, and Charles E. Snyder. Photograph by Edwin L. Dodds

Pueblo School District Administration Building, 315 West Eleventh Street

Designed by Hurtig, Gardner, and Froelich and completed in 1979, the building includes an exterior mural by Ken Williams. Photograph by Edwin L. Dodds

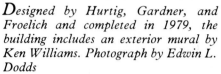

University of Southern Colorado

Located on the plains northeast of Pueblo the university began in 1933 as the Pueblo Junior College. By 1961 it had evolved into the Southern Colorado State College, and in 1975 university status was given. Photograph courtesy of University of South Colorado

The Kids Parade Sponsored by the Mesa Junction Merchants, a Favorite Event of Many Puebloans

Photograph by David R. Roscover, Pueblo Chieftain/Star-Journal

Guadalupe Dancers' Float

Fiesta days at the Colorado State Fair began in 1967 under the leadership of Henry Reyes and George Sandoval. In 1980 the Guadalupe Dancers' float won the Best Costumes award. Photograph courtesy of Chris McLean, Pueblo Chieftain/Star-Journal

Bibliography

Bauer, William H. et al. *Colorado Postal History: The Post Offices.* Crete, Nebraska: J-B Publishing Company, c. 1971.

Bryan, Ray. "Pueblo Family YMCA, 1889-1979." *Pueblo Family YMCA Fall Schedule, 1979.* Pueblo, Colorado: n.p., 1979.

Collins, Clara. "Career of Joseph Hitchens, Noted Colorado Artist." *Fine Arts Journal,* November, 1919, 291-93.

Curran, Terence. "Pueblo: The City that Couldn't Die." *Pueblo Star-Journal and Chieftain,* June 3, 1971.

Dallas, Sandra. *No More than Five in a Bed: Colorado Hotels in the Old Days.* Norman, Oklahoma: University of Oklahoma Press, 1967.

Darley, Alexander M. *The Passionists of the Southwest: Or the Holy Brotherhood.* Pueblo, Colorado: n.p., 1893.

Follansbee, Robert and Edward E. Jones. *The Arkansas River Flood of June 3-5, 1921.* Washington, D.C.: Government Printing Office, 1922.

From Mace's Hole, the Way It Was; to Beulah, the Way It Is. Colorado Springs, Beulah Historical Society, 1979.

Haley, James Evetts. *Charles Goodnight, Cowman and Plainsman.* Boston: Houston Mifflin, 1936.

Hall, Frank. *History of the State of Colorado.* Chicago: Blakely Printing Company, 1889-1895.

Hayes, Augustus Allen. *New Colorado and the Santa Fe Trail.* London: C. Kegan Paul and Company, 1881.

Helmers, Dow. *Tragedy at Eden.* Pueblo, Colorado: O'Brien Printing Company, 1971.

History of the Arkansas Valley, Colorado. . . . Chicago: O. L. Baskin and Company, 1881.

History of the St. Mary-Corwin School of Nursing, 1948-1964. Pueblo, Colorado: n.p., 1964.

Hoeglund, Harold A. *History of Pueblo College, Pueblo, Colorado, 1933-1963.* Pueblo, Colorado: Riverside Press, 1964.

Jackson, Donald, ed. *The Journals of Zebulon Montgomery Pike.* Norman, Oklahoma: University of Oklahoma Press, 1966.

Lecompte, Janet. *Pueblo, Hardscrabble and Greenhorn, the Upper Arkansas, 1832-1856.* Norman, Oklahoma: University of Oklahoma Press, 1978.

McIntyre, Katherine. *The Development of Commercial Banking in Pueblo County, Colorado.* Boulder, Colorado: Master's thesis, University of Colorado, 1935.

Machebeuf, J. P. *History of the Catholic Church in Colorado.* Denver, Colorado: C. J. Kelly Art Printing, 1947.

Miller, Nyle and Joseph W. Snell. *Great Gunfighters of the Kansas Cowtowns 1867-1886.* Lincoln, Nebraska: University of Nebraska Press, 1967.

Phelps, Harvey W. *A Brief Scan of the Minutes of the Pueblo County Medical Society 1881-1976.* Pueblo, Colorado: Pueblo County Medical Society, 1976.

Pueblo, Colorado, Its Resources and Developments: A Souvenir by the Daily Chieftain. Compiled by Dunn and Myers. Pueblo, Colorado, 1891.

"Pueblo West, Decade of Progress, 1969-1979." *Pueblo West Bulletin.* July, 1979.

Risley, James H. *How It Grew: A History of the Pueblo Public Schools.* Denver, Colorado: University of Denver Press, 1953.

Scamehorn, H. Lee. *Pioneer Steelmaker in the West: The Colorado Fuel and Iron Company 1872-1903.* Boulder, Colorado: Pruett Publishing Company, 1976.

Scott, Glenn R. *Historic Trail Maps of Pueblo 1° × 2° Quadrangle, Colorado.* Reston, Virginia: U.S. Geological Survey, 1975.

Stephenson, Norma J. *Pueblo, The People: An Oral History.* Boulder, Colorado: Western Interstate Commission for Higher Education, 1978.

Stone, Wilbur F. "Early Pueblo and the Men Who Made It." *Colorado Magazine,* 6:6, November, 1929, 199-210.

Taylor, Ralph. *Colorado South of the Border.* Denver, Colorado: Sage Books, 1963.

Whittaker, Milo Lee. *Pathbreakers and Pioneers of the Pueblo Region.* Pueblo, Colorado: Franklin Press, 1917.

Wilson, Elinor. *Jim Beckwourth.* Norman, Oklahoma: University of Oklahoma Press, 1972.

Wyant, Walter. *The Colorado Giant or Solid Muldoon.* Pueblo, Colorado: A Discover Pueblo Project, 1980.

X-Ray Pueblo. Pueblo, Colorado: League Club of Business and Professional Women, 1968.

Index